PENGUIN
SELF-
STARTERS

GU00801979

Accounting

Noel Trimming is a graduate of London University and a
Chartered Secretary. He spent twenty-eight years in Zimbabwe,
working first as a Civil Servant and then as Economist to the
Chamber of Mines. Since 1980 he has been teaching at Davies's
College, London, where he is Senior Accounting Tutor in the
Management Studies Department.

He is married, with four children, and lives in Merstham,
Surrey.

SERIES EDITORS: Stephen Coote and Bryan Loughrey

Accounting

Noel Trimming
B.Sc.(Econ.), ACIS

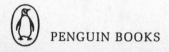

PENGUIN BOOKS

PENGUIN BOOKS

Published by the Penguin Group
27 Wrights Lane, London W8 5TZ, England
Viking Penguin Inc., 40 West 23rd Street, New York, New York 10010, USA
Penguin Books Australia Ltd, Ringwood, Victoria, Australia
Penguin Books Canada Ltd, 2801 John Street, Markham, Ontario, Canada L3R 1B4
Penguin Books (NZ) Ltd, 182–190 Wairau Road, Auckland 10, New Zealand

Penguin Books Ltd, Registered Offices: Harmondsworth, Middlesex, England

First published 1988
10 9 8 7 6 5 4 3 2

Filmset in Linotron 202 Melior

Typeset, printed and bound in Great Britain by
Hazell Watson & Viney Limited
Member of BPCC plc
Aylesbury, Bucks, England

For my wife, Patricia,
and Paul, Stephen, John and Helen

Contents

8 Contents

Preface

This book is addressed primarily to the general reader. It is intended for people who wish to find out something about accounting without having to acquire a specialist's knowledge of it. But I very much hope that it will also be found useful by students who are beginning, or contemplating, a course of studies in which accounting will play a large part and who would like to have some preliminary idea of what to expect. For this reason my aim throughout the book has been to present a perspective, or long view, of accounting which stresses its unity and consistency and avoids undue differentiation of topics. I have also been at some pains not to use technical language until the terminology has been adequately explained.

Readers should find enough in the opening chapters to enable them to master double entry and profit calculation, particularly if they work conscientiously through the exercises – which I strongly urge them to do. Accounting is an art; like any other art, it requires practice as a condition of competence. The later chapters, starting roughly with the Partnership section of Chapter 6, have had to be treated in a more general way because of the increasing complexity of the subject matter and the consequent need to distinguish more rigorously between principle and detail. Much that is interesting has had to be omitted, but this radical cutting back of the trees should at least make possible a clearer view of the wood.

My thanks are due to Mr Riad Izhar and Mrs Ranee Harris, both of Davies's College, to whom I am indebted for a number of helpful discussions, and to Mr Henry Curtis, FCA, for the generous attention and advice he gave me at the proof-reading stage.

Introduction

Most text books, and even some dictionaries, define accounting in terms which are meaningful only to people who already know a good deal about the subject. Something more direct, and at the same time more general, is required for our purposes. We shall start therefore by saying that accounting is 'an art or discipline which has as its object the profitable and responsible use of goods and money'.

The need for the correct use of money, and the goods which it represents, is something with which everybody is familiar. Wherever money transactions take place some form of accounting will be involved, even in the least developed societies; in our sophisticated culture, it is taken for granted that mature men and women will have a reasonable understanding at least of their own financial affairs. The differences between the simple accounting which this entails and the complex accounting systems which serve industry, commerce and finance are really differences of scale rather than of principle. Quite a lot may be learnt about what accounting is, and what it does, by considering how people go about their daily affairs.

A housewife, for example, has a certain income at her disposal each month, to provide for her family's needs, and she will wish to spend this money as wisely as possible. In order to do this, she may decide to construct a household budget. This will mean that she will have to (a) record as clearly and accurately as she can whatever money she receives or spends. Then she will have to (b) find some way of bringing these separate items of information together each month in a statement, or report, which will tell her whether or not the family income is sufficient for its needs. Her husband will have to (c) be able to interpret and understand these calculations. They will then, presumably, together decide (d) what to do about their affairs in the next period. Finally, they will have to (e) ensure that whatever plan they have made is reflected in their actual receipts and expenditure. In this very ordinary process there can be found the elements of five major accounting functions: Recording, Reporting, Interpretation, Prediction and Control. The rest of this book will be devoted to examining how these functions are put to use in the business world.

Before we proceed to this, however, it will be necessary for us to take note of the fundamental accounting rule of *objectivity*. A husband and wife may well have different views on the values they attach to the items in their budget, but usually after discussion, and perhaps persuasion, they will arrive at a working agreement on these matters. Consensus of this kind is not so easily achieved in the accountancy profession. In order to ensure the objectivity, or emphasis on ascertainable fact (as opposed to *subjectivity*, or reliance on personal opinion) without which the communication of financial information would be impossible, it has been found necessary to lay down a code of *accounting concepts*, which have themselves been modified by *accounting conventions*. A number of these concepts and conventions will be explained in the chapters which follow, in the context in which they naturally arise.

1 The Recording Function

1 The Elements of Recording

The need for intelligibility and accuracy

Accounting is, among other things, the 'language of business'. It is the medium through which ordinary business transactions are conducted even when, as often happens, the parties concerned are unaware of the precise meaning of the terms they are using. Traders frequently use words like 'profit', 'expense' and 'depreciation' etc. quite freely, on the assumption that people will know what they mean without further explanation. Each of these words in fact has a technical significance which is by no means identical with the meaning it has acquired from normal vernacular usage. Unless traders understand this and allow for it, they will sooner or later find themselves in serious difficulty. Accounting, if it is to be an *intelligible* means of business communication, requires strict attention to the meaning of words and the context in which they are used.

Communication must not only be intelligible if it is to be effective; it must also be *accurate*. There is no point in conveying a message, however clear it may be, if the information it contains is wrong. Business information will only be correct, and capable of being *proved* to be correct, if it is derived from a reliable record of the daily transactions upon which business is based. The first function of modern accounting is, therefore, to provide an intelligible and accurate recording system.

The double entry system

A normal trading transaction in itself is a simple matter: value in the form of goods or services is given in exchange for value in the form of money. But there are a number of things the trader must know and record about each transaction if he is to keep himself fully informed about the state of his business. Was the transaction, for example, a sale or was it a purchase? What was the value of the transaction? Has money been paid or has an obligation to pay been incurred? The recording method which has been developed by accountants to meet these needs is known as the **double entry system**. The term 'double entry' reflects the two-sided nature of each transaction – its 'giving' aspect and its 'receiving' aspect – and the need to take account of both of these aspects. If I sell goods worth £200 to Mr Brown on credit terms, I need to record the fact that I have 'given' the goods and he has 'received' them, in the sense that value has passed *from* me *to* him. When he pays me the £200, I must also record the passing of money *from* him (as 'giving') *to* me (as 'receiving'). Failure to record any of these aspects would have troublesome consequences for my business.

The double entry system adopts as its basic unit of record the **ledger account**, a term which is easier to demonstrate than to define. Assume that a shopkeeper has sold a customer a box of chocolates worth £5 and that the customer has paid for his purchase in cash. The effect of this transaction has been to add £5 *to* the shopkeeper's cash resources, an increase which has arisen *from* the sales activity of the firm. Now, in accounting, the recording of the 'receiving' aspect of the transaction – roughly speaking, the 'to' side – is designated **debiting**, while the recording of the 'giving' aspect – or 'from' side – is called **crediting**. This is done on two halves of a vertically divided page, the left-hand side being reserved for debit entries and the right-hand side for credit entries. In the case we are considering, it is the **Cash Account** – the ledger account reflecting the cash resources of the firm – which is recorded as receiving, and the **Sales Account** – the ledger account reflecting the sales activity of the firm – which is recorded as giving. Two separate ledger accounts are required, thus:

(*Debit side*)   (*Credit side*)

Cash

	£		£
Mar 1 Sales	5.00		

Sales

	£		£
		Mar 1 Cash	5.00

Now assume that, instead of paying cash, the customer, whom we shall call J. Smith, arranged with the shopkeeper to pay later. Obviously the Cash Account did not benefit from the transaction immediately, and the accounts must therefore be presented differently. J. Smith himself is shown as having received the value and an account is opened in his name.

J. Smith

	£		£
Mar 1 Sales	5.00		

The entry in the Sales Account is the same as before, except that the name 'J. Smith' appears in place of the word 'cash'.

Sales

	£		£
		Mar 1 J. Smith	5.00

Notice at this point that every ledger account automatically records the name of the ledger account in which the opposite side of the transaction, i.e. the corresponding debit or credit, has been entered.

Mr Smith will remain a debtor of the firm (that is, his account will continue to show a debit entry) until he pays the amount owing. Suppose that he does this on 5 March. The cash resources of the firm are increased by £5, so the Cash Account is now debited, exactly as it would have been if the £5 had been paid at the time of the sale, except that the name 'J. Smith' appears instead of the word 'Sales'. J. Smith as the giver of value is credited. The full record now appears as:

	Sales	
	£	£
	Mar 1 J. Smith	5.00

	J. Smith	
	£	£
Mar 1 Sales	5.00	Mar 5 Cash	5.00

	Cash	
	£	£
Mar 5 J. Smith	5.00		

No new entry is made in the Sales Account as it is not affected by Mr Smith's payment on 5 March. In J. Smith's account, the double line under the debit and credit entries indicates that the account now balances, i.e. that the debit and credit entries are exactly equal. Mr Smith no longer has any obligation to the firm; his account is closed and will be removed from the books unless similar transactions are expected in the near future.

All sales activity depletes the firm's stock of goods for sale, and in due course the shopkeeper will have to replenish his stocks. If he purchases £200 worth on 6 March for cash, the ledger account entries will be:

	Cash	
	£	£
	Mar 6 Purchases	200

	Purchases	
	£	£
Mar 6 Cash	200		

The Cash Account gives the value, in the sense of paying £200, and the firm's *purchased* goods receive the value, in the form of an increase of stock worth £200.

Unless the shopkeeper has only recently commenced trading, it is improbable that he would pay for his purchases in cash; it is more likely that he would have a credit arrangement with his wholesaler. Let us suppose then that he purchased the goods on 6 March and paid for them on 31 March. Under these circumstances, the wholesaler's account would be credited, instead of the Cash Account, and would be debited with the payment in due course.

XYZ Wholesalers

		£			£
Mar 31	Cash	200	Mar 6 Purchases		200

Purchases

		£		£
Mar 6	XYZ Wholesalers	200		

Cash

	£			£
		Mar 31	XYZ Wholesalers	200

What happens if, instead of paying the full amount, the shop-keeper arranges to pay in two instalments of £100 each, the first of which is paid on 31 March? The records would then show:

XYZ Wholesalers

		£			£
Mar 31	Cash	100	Mar 6 Purchases		200
	Balance carried down	100			
		200			200
			Apr 1 Balance brought down		100

Purchases

		£		£
Mar 6	XYZ Wholesalers	200		

Cash

	£			£
		Mar 31	XYZ Wholesalers	100

The term 'balance carried down' (usually written as 'balance c/d') on the debit side of XYZ Wholesalers' account indicates that the amount entered on the debit side is lower than that appearing on the credit side by £100; and the term 'balance brought down' (or 'balance

b/d') means that, because of this difference, £100 is still owing to
XYZ Wholesalers on 1 April.

A trader engages in transactions other than merely the purchase
and sale of goods. He must also record **expense** payments such as
wages, rent and electricity. A shopkeeper who pays £50 in wages is
giving value in the form of cash and *receiving value* in the form of
a labour service. He therefore *credits* his Cash Account and *debits*
the Wages Account (the most convenient way of recording the cost
of labour):

Cash Account			
	£		£
		Mar 7 Wages	50

Wages Account			
	£		£
Mar 7 Cash	50		

Other expense payments are dealt with in precisely the same way.

Let us now summarize what we have been discussing by recording
the first week's transactions of a trader, Mr T. Jones, who has just
commenced business. (The 'action required' column is not part of
the recording process; it is included here only for explanatory purposes.)

Example 1.1.

	Transaction	Action required
March 1	Mr Jones invested £1000 in the business	debit Cash, credit Capital
	He used £200 of this money to purchase goods for sale	debit Purchases, credit Cash
" 2	Goods were sold for cash: £50	debit Cash, credit Sales
	Goods were sold on credit to M. Brown: £25	debit M. Brown, credit Sales
" 3	The month's rent was paid in advance: £200	debit Rent, credit Cash
	Cash Sales recorded: £100	debit Cash, credit Sales
	Goods were sold to J. Black on credit: £50	debit J. Black, credit Sales

" 4 Goods purchased on credit   debit Purchases, credit
       from A. Green: £300   A. Green
" 5 Cash Sales recorded: £150   debit Cash, credit Sales
       Credit Sales to J. White: £40   debit J. White, credit
                                     Sales

       Cash received from   debit Cash, credit
          M. Brown: £25   M. Brown

The first transaction requires a little further explanation. In terms of
one of the basic concepts of accounting – the **business entity** concept
– the owner and his business are regarded as separate entities. This
avoids the complication of having to disentangle the owner's private
transactions (household expenses, etc.) from those of the business
in order to arrive at the profit made by the business. Because of this
distinction between the owner and the business, it is necessary to
open an account for the owner in the firm's books. By convention,
this is called the **Capital Account**.

Capital

	£			£
		Mar	1 Cash	1 000

Cash

		£			£
Mar	1 Capital	1 000	Mar	1 Purchases	200
"	2 Sales	50	"	3 Rent	200
"	3 Sales	100		Balance c/d	925
"	5 Sales	150			
	M. Brown	25			
		1 325			1 325
Mar	7 Balance b/d	925			

Purchases

		£			£
Mar	1 Cash	200	Mar	5 Balance c/d	500
"	4 A. Green	300			
		500			500
Mar	7 Balance b/d	500			

Sales

		£				£
Mar 5 Balance c/d		415	Mar	2	Cash	50
					M. Brown	25
			"	3	Cash	100
					J. Black	50
			"	5	Cash	150
					J. White	40
		415				415
			Mar	7	Balance b/d	415

Rent

	£		£
Mar 3 Cash	200		

M. Brown

	£		£
Mar 2 Sales	25	Mar 5 Cash	25

J. Black

	£		£
Mar 3 Sales	50		

A. Green

	£		£
		Mar 4 Purchases	300

J. White

	£		£
Mar 5 Sales	40		

This completes the ledger account entries for the week. But how can we be sure that the entries have been correctly made? One method of checking is to draw up what is known as a **trial balance**. This is simply a list of the balances in the accounts, presented in two columns to demonstrate that the total of the debits equals the total of the credits.

Trial Balance

	Dr	Cr
	£	£
Capital		1000
Cash	925	
Purchases	500	
Sales		415
J. Black	50	
J. White	40	
Rent	200	
A. Green		300
	1715	1715

The totals agree at £1715, so it can be assumed that the requirements
of the double entry system have been met. The method of correcting
errors disclosed by the trial balance is discussed in Chapter 3.

Exercises*

Before starting, remember:
- (a) Every time a debit entry is made, there must be a corresponding credit entry made in some other account.
- (b) No account should be balanced before the last entry is
  made for the period.
- (c) The trial balance includes only balances still outstanding
  at the end of the period.

Exercise 1.1.   H. Carruthers commenced business on 1 August by
investing £5000 in his business. His firm then purchased
£1500 worth of goods for resale on the same day. His transactions for the rest of the week were:

August 2   Cash sales: £50
              Credit sale to J. D'Arcy: £250
      "   3   Rent paid in cash: £400
              Cash sales: £150
              Credit sale to B. Cholmondeley: £90
      "   4   Credit sale to S. Ponsonby: £200
              and to R. Beauchamp: £65
              Goods purchased on credit from

* Solutions to the Exercises can be found at the end of the book, beginning
   on page 147.

Mayfair Wholesalers: £500
Cash sales: £400
"   5   Cash received from J. D'Arcy: £150
and from B. Cholmondeley: £90
Cash sales: £300

Enter these transactions in the appropriate ledger accounts, balance the accounts where necessary and extract a trial balance as at 5 March.

Exercise 1.2.   On 1 September, B. Atman invested £6 000 in a retail shop and purchased goods worth £2 000 on credit from S. Uperman. During his first week of trading his transactions were:

September 2   Cash sales: £550
Credit sales S. Piderman: £120
"   3   Cash sales: £700
Rent paid in cash: £400
Insurance paid in cash: £300
"   4   Cash sales: £250
S. Piderman paid: £120
"   5   Cash sales: £300
Wages paid in cash: £100
The firm paid S. Uperman: £1 000
Credit sales C. Marvel: £200

Enter the transaction in the ledgers, balance the accounts and extract a trial balance.

2 The System in Practice

The ledger

The ledger account, as we have seen, is the basic unit of record. It is now necessary to consider what exactly is meant by the word *ledger*. Accounts fall naturally into different categories according to whichever aspect of the firm's activity they reflect. In Example 1.1, the accounts for M. Brown, J. Black and T. White have a common purpose: they are accounts which record the indebtedness of individual customers arising from the *sales* activity of the firm. They will therefore be grouped together as separate pages (or cards, depending on whether a manual or mechanical system of recording is being used) in what is called the **Sales Ledger** (sometimes known as the Debtors' Ledger). A. Green's account reflects an obligation to pay on the part of the firm arising from its *purchasing* activity and will therefore appear among the accounts of other suppliers in the **Purchases Ledger** (sometimes called the Creditors' Ledger). These arrangements have the obvious advantage of enabling the owner and his staff to locate individual accounts quickly and easily. They also greatly assist the calculation of totals of debts outstanding and amounts due to creditors. Ledgers are therefore simply convenient divisions of the full set of accounts. They may be bound volumes or, more usually nowadays, sections of a card system. The number of ledgers a firm maintains will be decided by its size and its type of trading activity. It may be taken for granted that most firms will have at least a Sales Ledger, a Purchases Ledger and a General Ledger. Many firms also use a Nominal Ledger, for expense accounts, and a Real Ledger, for asset accounts, instead of including these accounts in the General Ledger, as would otherwise be the case.

Books of original entry

The method of recording which has been described so far is perfectly correct bookkeeping in principle, but it would be a cumbersome system to operate in practice. In order to reduce the number of entries and to maintain an accurate and readily accessible record of the information derived from the basic documents, a number of **books of original entry** or **subsidiary books** have been devised. Among these are the **Day Books**. The Day Books are not themselves part of the double entry system but are subsidiary to it. They provide the link between basic documents and ledger accounts.

The Sales Day Book

The Sales Day Book records the invoices issued to customers in order of date and invoice number:

Date	Name	Invoice No.	Folio	Amount
				£
Mar 15	R. Brown	5392	SL 18	68
" 17	H. Jones	5393	SL 32	114
" 19	F. Thompson	5394	SL 74	256
" 20	B. Clarke	5395	SL 25	95
		To Sales Account	GL 13	533

The amount on each invoice is taken individually to the debit of the personal account of the customer concerned; to indicate that this has been done, the number of the page, or *folio*, on which the customer's account appears in the Sales Ledger is inserted in the folio column of the Day Book. The total of the amount column in the Day Book is then credited to the Sales Account. In the example given above, it can be seen that the double entry requirements are met by one *credit* entry instead of four. The debit entries must of course be carried out individually because they refer to four separate debtors' accounts.

The Purchases Day Book

The Purchases Day Book is identical in format with the Sales Day
Book and records similar details regarding invoices *received* from
suppliers:

Date	Name	Invoice No.	Folio	Amount
				£
Mar 14	R. Macdonald	2393	PL 37	419
" 16	D. Cohen	387	PL 14	283
" 17	J. Fuller	1285	PL 18	55
" 20	B. Anderson	630	PL 3	93
		To Purchases Account	GL 12	850

The amounts due to individual suppliers are credited to their personal accounts in the Purchases Ledger and the total amount is debited to the Purchases Account.

The Returns Inwards Book and the Returns Outwards Book list the
transactions relating to returns.

Returns Inwards Book

Date	Name	Credit Note	Folio	Amount
				£
Mar 21	H. Jones	15	SL 32	29
" 23	F. Thompson	16	SL 74	87
	To Returns Inwards Account		GL 26	116

H. Jones and F. Thompson have 'given value' in the sense of return-
ing goods, which is equivalent to having paid for them. Their personal accounts in the Sales Ledger will be credited and they
themselves will be sent *credit notes* to indicate that this has been
done. The firm has 'received value' in the form of the goods returned
and its Returns Inwards Account will be debited with the total
amount.

Returns Outwards Book

Date	Name	Debit Note	Folio	Amount
				£
Mar 19	R. Macdonald	25	PL 37	58
" 24	B. Anderson	26	PL 3	17
	To Returns Outwards Account		GL 27	75

The firm has returned goods to R. Macdonald and B. Anderson, and their personal accounts will accordingly be debited with the value they have received. The firm's Returns Outwards Account is credited with the total amount.

In working with Day Books it is essential to bear in mind that the terms 'day book', 'account' and 'ledger' are distinct terms with different meanings. Thus a sales invoice is (1) recorded in the Sales *Day Book*; (2) then debited to the customer's account in the Sales *Ledger*; and (3) credited to the Sales *Account* in the General Ledger. This may seem confusing at this stage, but a little practice will quickly clarify the matter.

The Cash Book

The Cash Account and the Bank Account are both properly part of the General Ledger; however, because these accounts are in daily use, there are obvious advantages in locating them in a separate part of the accounting system where they can be quickly referred to without searching through what would otherwise be an extremely bulky General Ledger. Also, because there are frequent and continuing transactions between the Cash Account and the Bank Account in the form of deposits and withdrawals, it is helpful to keep the two in close proximity. The **Double Column Cash Book** does this by presenting the amounts debited to the Cash Account and the Bank Account in two adjacent columns, with a similar columnar arrangement for the credit amounts on the opposite side of the page. However, it is important to understand and remember that, while these two accounts are shown together in the Cash Book, they are, in fact, separate ledger accounts with their own balances brought down and carried down. The Cash Book is unique in accounting in that it is both a book of original entry and also two ledger accounts.

Let us examine a number of Cash Book entries and consider their meaning.

Cash Book

		Cash	Bank				Cash	Bank
		£	£				£	£
Mar 1	Capital	–	1000	Mar 1	Cash		–	200
	Bank	200	–	" 2	Purchases		–	300
" 2	Sales	50	–	" 3	Rent		–	200
" 3	Sales	100	–	" 5	Wages		100	–
" 5	Sales	150	–		Bank		200	–
	Cash	–	200		Balance c/d		200	525
	M. Brown	–	25					
		500	1225				500	1225
Mar 8	Balance b/d	200	525					

These entries record the following transactions:

March 1   The owner invests £1000 in the business by paying in a
                cheque to the firm's bank account
                (*debit Bank*, credit Capital)
                £200 is withdrawn for use by the business
                (*debit Cash*, credit Bank – the Bank Account is
                'giving' to the Cash Account)

"   2   Goods to the value of £300 are purchased by cheque –
                i.e. from the Bank Account
                (debit Purchases, *credit Bank*)
                Goods are sold for £50 in cash
                (*debit Cash*, credit Sales)

"   3   Rent £200 is paid by cheque
                (debit Rent, *credit Bank*)
                Cash sales £100
                (*debit Cash*, credit Sales)

"   5   £100 wages are paid in cash
                (debit Wages, *credit Cash*)
                Cash sales £150
                (*debit Cash*, credit Sales)
                A cheque for £25 is received from M. Brown

> (*debit Bank*, credit M. Brown – the Bank Account
> is receiving the cheque)

March 5   The firm deposits £200 in the bank

> (*debit Bank, credit Cash* – the Cash Account is 'giving'
> the Bank Account £200)

At close of business on Friday, 5 March, the total of cash received is seen to be £500 (the total of the debit column) but of this £200 has been deposited in the Bank and £100 spent on wages. This means that the credit entries in the Cash Account are short of the debit entries by the £200 remaining. This balance (shown against March 5 as *carried down*) is the amount of cash with which the firm will start the next week (shown on the debit side against March 8 as the balance *brought down*). Similarly, the Bank Account has received £1 225 but has spent £700, and a balance of £525 is carried down to the following week.

Few firms now use the Double Column Cash Book because so many business transactions are conducted on a credit basis, which means that account often has to be taken of **discounts allowed** and **discounts received** when payments are received or made. This is provided for by adding a third column to the debit side, for discounts allowed, and to the credit side for discounts received.

Cash Book (treble column)

		Discount	Cash	Bank			Discount	Cash	Bank
		£	£	£			£	£	£
Jun	1 Balance b/d	–	170	800	Jun	2 G. Grindlay	60	–	540
"	2 Sales	–	350	–		Rent	–	–	100
"	2 B. Barclay	20	–	380		C. Coop	20	–	180
"	3 Sales	–	400	–	"	3 Wages	–	100	–
"	4 L. Lloyd	25	–	475		Bank	–	600	–
"	5 Cash	–	–	600		Balance c/d	–	220	1435
		45	920	2255			80	920	2255
Jun	8 Balance b/d		220	1435					

Before B. Barclay's payment on 2 June, his account will have shown a debit balance of £400. As he is paying within the period stipulated for discount, he is allowed 5% discount, £20. He therefore sends in a cheque for £380 and the payment is credited to his personal account in the Sales Ledger. He must of course also be credited with the discount allowed, otherwise his account will show a £20 debit balance as still owing.

B. Barclay

	£			£
Jun 1 Balance b/d	400	Jun 2 Bank		380
		Discount		20
	400			400

G. Grindlay is one of the firm's suppliers and he allows 10% on bills paid within the agreed period. His account will have shown a credit balance brought down of £600 on 1 June. The firm therefore deducts £60 for discount received and pays him £540.

G. Grindlay

	£		£
Jun 1 Bank	540	Jun 1 Balance b/d	600
Discount	60		
	600		600

It will be seen that no balance is carried down or brought down in the discount columns of the Cash Book. This is because two separate accounts are concerned – the Discount Allowed Account and the Discount Received Account – and it is not good accounting practice to offset one against the other. The total of the Discount Allowed column is entered in the debit side of the Discount Allowed Account; and the total of the Discount Received column is entered on the credit side of the Discount Received Account (see below). Suppose that discounts totalling £542 have been allowed for the period 1 January to 31 May and that discounts totalling £680 have been received during the same period. The entries would appear as:

Discounts Allowed

	£		£
Jun 1 Balance b/d	542		
" 5 Sundry debtors	45		

Discounts Received

	£		£
		Jun 1 Balance b/d	680
		" 5 Sundry creditors	80

The word 'sundry' simply means 'some' or 'various'. If it is necessary to know the names of the personal accounts debited or credited with the opposite entries, this information can easily be obtained from the Cash Book, the book of original entry.

The Journal

The subsidiary books we have been considering record all the transactions concerned with the ordinary process of buying and selling. But there are occasions in accounting when entries are called for which cannot be routed through the Day Books. These entries may, for example, arise from the need (i) to correct errors, (ii) to record the purchase or sale of 'fixed assets', i.e. goods purchased for use within the business and not intended for resale, or (iii) to take account of a change in the circumstances of a debtor or a creditor. There are a number of other and more complicated uses of the journal which will be explained in later chapters.

A journal page is ruled in two columns; it records the double entry being made, together with a short narrative account of the circumstances which have given rise to it. Let us suppose that the sale to R. Brown on 15 March which appears in our Sales Day Book example above was incorrectly debited to R. Brand, who already owed the firm £40. Before the correcting entries, R. Brand's account will have appeared as:

			£			£
		R. Brand				SL 18
Mar	1	Balance b/d	40	Mar 31 Balance c/d		108
"	15	Sales	68			
			108			108
Apr	1	Balance b/d	108			

When the error is discovered – which will probably occur as the result of a query from Mr Brand about the amount appearing on his statement of account – it will be necessary to put through a correcting journal entry. By convention, the account to be debited is always shown first in the journal.

	Journal		JNL 23
	Folio	*Dr*	*Cr*
		£	£
Apr 6 R. Brown	SL 19	68	
R. Brand	SL 18		68
Correction of mis-posting of sales invoice 5392 dated 15 March.			

This information will be 'posted to' (or entered in) the two accounts concerned and proof of these entries will appear in the folio columns of the journal and the personal accounts.

	R. Brand		SL 18
	£		£
Apr 1 Balance b/d	108	Apr 6 R. Brown SL 19	68
		Balance c/d	40
	108		108
Apr 6 Balance b/d	40		

	R. Brown		SL 19
	£		£
Apr 6 R. Brand SL 18	68		

R. Brand's account now shows the amount correctly due from him, and he will be sent an amended statement of account.

Because of the double entry principle, the *totals* of the debit and credit columns in any one transfer will always be equal, but this does not mean that the *number* of debit and credit entries will necessarily be the same. A firm purchasing an office desk and a typewriter on credit from the same supplier will debit two asset accounts against a single credit entry:

	Dr	Cr
	£	£
Apr 15 Office Furniture	850	
Office Equipment	420	
ABC Furnishers		1 270
Purchase of office desk and typewriter as per supplier's invoice 05-639		

The journal is being used in this instance because, since the assets are not intended for resale and therefore are not 'purchases' in the technical sense in which accountants use the term, the transaction cannot be recorded in the Purchases Day Book. The significance of this will become clearer when we consider the Trading Account and the Balance Sheet in Chapters 4 and 6.

Transfers between personal accounts can take place for reasons other than the need to correct errors. When a woman customer marries and changes her name, the account appearing under her maiden name will be closed, by crediting it with the amount currently showing as the debit balance brought forward, and by debiting the amount to an account opened in her new name.

	Dr	Cr
	£	£
Jun 10 H. Thompson	53	
H. Green		53
Transfer of debit balance resulting from change of name – Miss H. Green to Mrs H. Thompson		

Example 2.1. The following balances appeared in the books of Mr A. Johnson at 31 March:

Debit: Shop fittings £500, Van £2 200, G. Allen £540, F. Barker £120, E. Carter £400, Bank £4 239, Cash £300, Returns Inwards £65, Discount Allowed £120, Purchases £3 500, Wages £820, Rent £300.

Credit: Capital £5 000, D. Edwards £700, E. Fanshaw £300, F. Gregory £120, Returns Outwards £44, Discount Received £240, Sales £6 700.

Transactions for the week 1–6 April were:

April 1   Goods purchased on credit from E. Fanshaw: £200
  (invoice 857/2)
  Cash sales: £150
  Credit sales: invoice 539 – G. Allen: £102
      invoice 540 – O. Mitchell: £247
  " 2   E. Carter paid his account by cheque less 5% discount
  Cash sales: £200
  Credit purchases: F. Gregory: £300 (invoice 321)
  " 3   Cash sales: £180
  Cash paid into bank: £500
  Returns Outwards: Debit Note no. 23, E. Fanshaw: £40
      24, F. Gregory: £105

" 4   The firm paid D. Edwards the amount due to him by cheque less 3% discount

        Cash sales: £220

        G. Allen paid in a cheque for £513, having deducted £27 discount

" 5   A shelving unit was purchased on credit for £250 from EFG Shop Fitters

        Cash sales: £170

" 6   Returns Inwards: G. Allen: £22 (Credit Note 39)

                                  E. Carter: £15 (Credit Note 40)

        Cash sales: £50

        Credit sale: invoice 541 – F. Burke: £470

        Wages paid in cash: £200

        £350 paid by cheque for rent

Record these transactions in the books of original entry, post them to the ledgers and extract a trial balance. Folio number entries may be omitted.

Solution

Dr   **Cash Book**   Cr

		Discount	Cash	Bank			Discount	Cash	Bank
		£	£	£			£	£	£
Apr	1 Balance b/d	–	300	4 239	Apr	3 Bank	–	500	–
	Sales	–	150	–	"	4 D. Edwards	21	–	679
"	2 E. Carter	20	–	380	"	6 Wages	–	200	–
	Sales	–	200	–		Rent	–	–	350
"	3 Sales	–	180	–		Balance c/d	–	570	4 603
	Cash	–	–	500					
"	4 Sales	–	220	–					
	G. Allen	27	–	513					
"	5 Sales	–	170	–					
"	6 Sales	–	50	–					
		47	1 270	5 632			21	1 270	5 632
Apr	8 Balance b/d		570	4 603					

Sales Day Book

Date	Invoice No.	Name	Amount
			£
Apr 1	539	G. Allen	102
	540	O. Mitchell	247
" 6	541	F. Burke	470
			819

Purchases Day Book

Date	Invoice No.	Name	Amount
			£
Apr 1	857/2	E. Fanshaw	200
" 2	321	F. Gregory	300
			500

Returns Outwards Book

Date	Debit Note No.	Name	Amount
			£
Apr 3	23	E. Fanshaw	40
	24	F. Gregory	105
			145

Returns Inwards Book

Date	Credit Note No.	Name	Amount
			£
Apr 6	39	G. Allen	22
	40	E. Carter	15
			37

Journal

		Dr	Cr
		£	£
Apr 5	Shop Fittings	250	
	EFG Shop Fitters		250
	Purchase of asset on credit		

General Ledger

Capital

	£		£
		Apr 1 Balance b/d	5 000

Vans

	£		£
Apr 1 Balance b/d	2 200		

Shop Fittings

	£		£
Apr 1 Balance b/d	500	Apr 6 Balance c/d	750
" 5 EFG Shop Fitters	250		
	750		750
Apr 6 Balance b/d	750		

Sales

			£					£
Apr	6	Balance c/d	8489	Apr	1	Balance b/d		6700
				"	6	Sundry Debtors		819
				"	1	Cash		150
				"	2	Cash		200
				"	3	Cash		180
				"	4	Cash		220
				"	5	Cash		170
				"	6	Cash		50
			8489					8489
				Apr	8	Balance b/d		8489

Purchases

			£				£
Apr	1	Balance b/d	3500	Apr	6	Balance c/d	4000
"	2	Sundry Creditors	500				
			4000				4000
Apr	8	Balance b/d	4000				

Returns Inwards

			£				£
Apr	1	Balance b/d	65	Apr	6	Balance c/d	102
"	6	Sundry Debtors	37				
			102				102
Apr	8	Balance b/d	102				

Returns Outwards

			£				£
Apr	6	Balance c/d	189	Apr	1	Balance b/d	44
				"	6	Sundry Creditors	145
			189				189
				Apr	8	Balance b/d	189

Discounts Allowed

			£				£
Apr	1	Balance b/d	120	Apr	6	Balance c/d	167
		Sundry Debtors	47				
			167				167
Apr	8	Balance b/d	167				

Discounts Received

		£				£
Apr 6	Balance c/d	261	Apr 1	Balance b/d		240
		—	" 6	Sundry Creditors		21
		261				261
			Apr 8	Balance b/d		261

EFG Shop Fitters

	£			£
		Apr 5	Shop Fittings	250

Wages

		£			£
Apr 1	Balance b/d	820	Apr 6	Balance c/d	1020
" 6	Cash	200			—
		1020			1020
Apr 8	Balance b/d	1020			

Rent

		£			£
Apr 1	Balance b/d	300	Apr 6	Balance c/d	650
" 6	Bank	350			—
		650			650
Apr 8	Balance b/d	650			

Sales Ledger
G. Allen

		£			£
Apr 1	Balance b/d	540	Apr 4	Bank	513
	Sales	102		Discount	27
			" 6	Returns Inwards	22
				Balance c/d	80
		—			—
		642			642
Apr 8	Balance b/d	80			

F. Barker

		£		£
Apr 1	Balance b/d	120		

E. Carter

			£				£
Apr	1	Balance b/d	400	Apr	2	Bank	380
"	8	Balance c/d	15			Discount	20
				"	6	Returns Inwards	15
			415				415
				Apr	8	Balance b/d	15

O. Mitchell

			£				£
Apr	6	Sales	247				

F. Burke

			£				£
Apr	6	Sales	470				

Purchases Ledger
D. Edwards

			£				£
Apr	4	Bank	679	Apr	1	Balance b/d	700
		Discount Received	21				
			700				700

E. Fanshaw

			£				£
Apr	3	Returns Outwards	40	Apr	1	Balance b/d	300
"	6	Balance c/d	460			Purchases	200
			500				500
				Apr	8	Balance b/d	460

F. Gregory

			£				£
Apr	3	Returns Outwards	105	Apr	1	Balance b/d	120
"	6	Balance c/d	315	"	2	Purchases	300
			420				420
				Apr	8	Balance b/d	315

Trial Balance

	Dr	Cr
	£	£
Cash	570	
Bank	4603	
Capital		5000
Vans	2200	
Shop Fittings	750	
Sales		8489
Purchases	4000	
Returns Inwards	102	
Returns Outwards		189
Discounts Allowed	167	
Discounts Received		261
EFG Shopfitters		250
Wages	1020	
Rent	650	
G. Allen	80	
F. Barker	120	
E. Carter		15
O. Mitchell	247	
F. Burke	470	
E. Fanshaw		460
F. Gregory		315
	14979	14979

Exercise

Exercise 2.1.   The trial balance for Sherwood Stores on 1 September 1985 was as follows:

	Dr	Cr
	£	£
Capital		14000
Bank	8000	
Cash	900	
Vehicles	5000	
Office Equipment	1000	
Sales		16000
Purchases	11000	
Returns Inwards	770	
Returns Outwards		580
Discounts Allowed	1830	
Discounts Received		950
R. Hood	540	
L. John	880	
M. Miller	340	
F. Tuck		1250
W. Scarlet		620
A. Adale		150
Wages	1700	
Insurance	990	
Rent	600	
	33550	33550

During the week ending 5 September, the following transactions were recorded:

September 1   Cash sales: £500
Credit sales:
     invoice 458 – R. Hood: £400
              459 – A. Sheriff: £650

"   2   L. John paid his account by cheque less
     5% discount
Cash sales: £450
Rent paid in cash: £100
Cash paid into the bank: £800

"   3   Credit sales:
     invoice 460 – M. Miller: £300
Paid F. Tuck £1 125 by cheque after
     deducting 10% discount
Credit purchases:
     F. Tuck: £500 (invoice 928)
     W. Scarlet: £300 (invoice 062)
Goods returned by:
     R. Hood: £80 (Credit note 57)
     A. Sheriff: £50 (Credit note 58)
Cash sales: £300

"   4   R. Hood paid his account by cheque:
     £513, having been allowed £27
     discount
Cash sales: £270
Paid W. Scarlet by cheque: £620 – no
     discount due
Goods returned to:
     F. Tuck: £17 (Debit note 104)
     A. Adale: £23 (Debit note 105)

"   5   Cash paid into bank: £500
Paid wages in cash: £600
Cash sales: £350
Bought a typewriter on credit for office
     use from Nottingham Office Supplies:
     £400 (Invoice 781/X)

Record these transactions in the books of original entry, post them to the ledger and extract a trial balance as at the close of business on 5 September 1985.

3 Checking and Correcting the Records

Errors in the trial balance

We have seen in Chapter 1 that one useful method of testing the correctness of ledger entries is to extract a trial balance. If a difference appears between the totals of the debits and credits, the error (or errors) must of course be traced by referring back to the original documentation and to the books of original entry. Suppose that in Example 1.1 the trial balance had appeared as:

	Dr	Cr
	£	£
Capital		1 000
Cash	925	
Purchases	500	
Sales		415
J. White	40	
A. Green		300
	1 465	1 715

The difference of £250 between the two columns indicates that ledger entries have been either omitted or posted to the wrong side of the ledger. From the set of transactions set out in the Example, it is easy to trace the two errors concerned:

    (i) the sale to J. Black (£50) has been correctly recorded in the Sales Account but the corresponding debit entry in the debtor's account has not been effected;

    (ii) the payment of £200 rent has not been debited to the Rent Account.

The next step is to enter these missing items in the correct accounts, that is to debit the account of J. Black and the Rent Account. The obvious way to do this might seem to be simply to insert the correct entry, with a note in the ledger indicating that it had been omitted and that the omission was now being rectified. But this procedure, which would amount to attempting to correct the original breach of the double-entry system principle by another breach of the same principle, would leave the whole recording system open to fraud. It is in order to prevent this kind of abuse and to preserve the integrity of the double entry system that the **Suspense Account** has been developed.

This technique involves treating the difference between the two sides as if it were itself a balance in an account. This balance is, of course, the sum of the missing amounts (in our example, J. Black £50 and Rent £200) and the account is, as it were, holding ('suspending') these amounts until they can be legitimately transferred by journal entry to the correct accounts. The account is opened as soon as it is discovered that the trial balance does not balance, thus:

Trial Balance

	Dr	Cr
	£	£
Capital		1 000
Cash	925	
Purchases	500	
Sales		415
J. White	40	
A. Green		300
Suspense Account	250	
	1715	1715

and in the ledger:

Suspense Account

	£		£
Trial Balance error 250			

When the errors have been discovered and the accounts concerned identified, correcting entries are put through the journal:

Journal

	Dr	Cr
	£	£
1. J. Black	50	
Suspense		50
Correction of the omission to post Sales invoice no. A5793 to debtor's account		

	Dr	Cr
2. Rent	200	
Suspense		200
Correction of the omission to post cheque no. 73259 to the Rent Account		

These journal entries would be posted to the ledger accounts as:

J. Black

	£		£
Suspense	50		

Rent

	£		£
Suspense	200		

Suspense

	£		£
Trial Balance		J. Black	50
error	250	Rent	200
	250		250

The balance on the Suspense Account disappears, having been transferred to the correct accounts, and the trial balance now automatically balances, with the introduction of new balances for J. Black and Rent.

Not all trial balance adjustments are as simple as this. Suppose that in addition to the errors already in the Rent Account and in J. Black's account, the credit balance in J. Green's account appeared as £30 instead of £300, again because of a posting error. The original totals of the trial balance columns in this case would show £1 465 debit and £1 445 credit; that is, the opening balance in the Suspense Account would be a credit balance of £20 (the amount by which the credit total falls short of the debit total). The effect of the correcting journal entries on the Suspense Account would be:

Suspense Account

	£		£
J. Green	270	Trial Balance error	20
		J. Black	50
		Rent	200
	270		270

All errors have now been corrected and the trial balance totals will agree at £1715.

Errors not involving trial balance totals

Not all corrections of errors utilize the Suspense Account, which is a device designed specifically to deal with errors resulting in differences between debit and credit entries. Errors of other kinds fall into four separate categories:

(a) **Errors of commission.** An example of this would be the case we considered when discussing the Journal, in which a sale to R. Brown was incorrectly debited to the account of another customer, R. Brand. All that was required to correct this error was the journal entry described on page 31, transferring the debit from R. Brand's account to R. Brown's account.

(b) **Errors of omission.** These arise when a transaction is completely omitted from the firm's books. If R. Brown's sales invoice for some reason had not been recorded in the Sales Day Book, the effect would have been that the total sales posted to the credit side of the Sales Account would have been short by £68 and, of course, R. Brown's account in the Sales Ledger would not have been debited. The entries will now be made by a simple journal transaction:

Journal

	Dr	Cr
	£	£
R. Brown	68	
Sales Account		68

Correction of omission to record invoice 5392 dated March 15 in Sales Day Book

Notice that no attempt is made to change the entries in the Sales Day Book. Only the Journal and the Ledger accounts are involved.

(c) **Errors of original entry.** These are caused by a misreading and consequent misposting of the amount involved on both sides of a double-entry transaction. Suppose that the amount on R. Brown's invoice had been recorded in the Sales Day Book as £86 instead of £68; R. Brown would of course have been overcharged £18 and the Sales Account would have been overcredited with the same amount. The correcting journal transfer therefore *debits* the Sales Account and *credits* R. Brown. (A credit entry offsets, or reduces, a debit balance and vice versa, just as a minus offsets, or reduces, a plus.)

Journal

		Dr	Cr
		£	£
Apr 2	Sales	18	
	R. Brown		18
	Correction of error arising from misreading of invoice 5392		

Sales Ledger
R. Brown

		£			£
Mar 15	Sales	86	Apr 2	Sales	18
				Balance c/d	68
		86			86
Apr 2	Balance b/d	68			

General Ledger
Sales

		£			£
Apr 2	R. Brown	18	Mar 15	Sundry Debtors	551
	Balance c/d	533			
		551			551
			Apr 2	Balance b/d	533

(d) **Errors of principle** occur when one side of a transaction is entered, not merely in the wrong account, but in the wrong *kind* of account. We have already had occasion to notice that the purchase and sale of fixed assets are treated differently from the purchase and sale of trade goods. If the sale debited to R. Brown had been of a micro-computer which had formed part of the firm's office equipment and was now being disposed of as surplus to the firm's needs, then the amount should not have been entered into the Sales Account but credited instead to a special Disposal of Office Equipment Account. (Disposal of Assets Accounts are explained in the section on Depreciation in Chapter 5.) The error therefore is a breach of *principle*. The journal entries required for correction will be:

Journal

	Dr	Cr
	£	£
Sales	68	
Disposal of Office Equipment		68
Correction of error of principle arising from crediting of proceeds of sale of Office Equipment on March 15 to Sales Account		

Although the correction procedures we have discussed are all that is necessary to correct the ledger entries themselves, further adjustments will be necessary if the incorrect entries have already been taken into the calculation of profit.

Example 3.1.   T. Spencer has balanced his books for the month and has extracted a trial balance. Unfortunately, the two columns do not balance, the debit column totalling £3 885 and the credit column £4 192. On checking his records, he discovers the following errors:

1. A credit purchase to the value of £105 from Jones & Son has been credited to the account of H. Jones.
2. A sale of goods worth £550 to J. Martin has been debited to his account as £55.
3. An invoice relating to a purchase of goods worth £600 from T. White had been mislaid and no entry has been made in the books.
4. A sale to M. Thompson has been correctly debited to his account as £388 but entered in the Sales account as £200.
5. A payment of £230 for vehicle maintenance expenses has been debited to the Motor Vehicles Account.
6. A sale of goods to W. Smith for £800 has been posted to his account and to the Sales Account as £300.

Show the journal entries necessary to correct these errors and enter and balance the Suspense Account.

Solution

Journal

	Dr	Cr
	£	£
1 H. Jones	105	
Jones & Son		105
Correction of error of commission: Purchase invoice 6817E from Jones & Son		
2 J. Martin	495	
Suspense Account		495
Correction of misposting of Sales invoice S164		
3 Purchases	600	
T. White		600
Correction of error of omission: Purchases invoice X5350 from T. White		
4 Suspense	188	
Sales		188
Correction of misposting of Sales invoice S197		
5 Vehicle maintenance expenses	230	
Motor vehicles		230
Correction of error of principle		
6 W. Smith	500	
Sales		500
Correction of error of original entry: Sales invoice S251		

Suspense Account

	£		£
Trial Balance error	307	J. Martin	495
Sales	188		
	495		495

Control Accounts

Most modern firms conduct the bulk of their business on credit terms, and entries in the Sales Ledger and Purchases Ledger therefore take up a large part of the time spent in recording transactions. In the interest both of good customer relations and of business efficiency generally, it is important that this recording should be accurate. This is the purpose of the Sales Ledger and the Purchases Ledger Control Accounts.

As we have already seen, in every credit sale the debtor's personal account is debited and the Sales Account is credited. It follows, therefore, that the total amount of the sales debited to customers' accounts within any particular period must, because of the double-entry principle, equal the total amount of sales credited to the Sales Account for the same period. We know also that when a customer pays his debt, his personal account in the Sales Ledger is credited and the Cash Book is debited. It follows again that the total payments credited to debtors' accounts will equal the total debtors' payments debited to the Cash Book. The same is true of discounts: the sum of discounts allowed credited to the customers' accounts will always equal the total amount debited to the Discounts Allowed Account. This equality of totals provides a very useful check on the numerical accuracy of postings to customers' accounts. By bringing the totals together in a single account – the Sales Ledger Control Account – it is possible to calculate the debtors' figure at the end of a period without reference to the balances extracted from the Sales Ledger. The Purchases Ledger Control Account is constructed on exactly the same principles.

Although they are not extracted from the Sales and Purchases ledgers, Control Accounts are really summaries of debtors' and creditors' accounts. If this is borne in mind, the writing up of the actual Controls becomes perfectly straightforward, because any difficulty about deciding where a particular entry should go can always be resolved by considering where the equivalent entry would be put in an individual debtor's, or creditor's, personal account.

If, for example, J. Thompson owes the firm £500 at the beginning of May, purchases further goods to the value of £300 during the month, and then pays £500 less 5% discount on 31 May, his account, as we know, will look like this:

J. Thompson

	£		£
May 1 Balance b/d	500	May 31 Bank	475
" 10 Sales	300	Discount Allowed	25
		Balance c/d	300
	800		800
Jun 1 Balance b/d	300		

If all the firm's debtors, including Mr Thompson, between them owed £15 000 at the beginning of the month and bought a further £60 000 worth of goods during the month, and paid £54 000 after deducting £2 500 discount, the Sales Ledger Control Account – provided all the transactions had been correctly posted – would be shown as:

Sales Ledger Control Account

	£		£
May 1 Balance b/d	15 000	Bank	54 000
Sales	60 000	Discounts	
		Allowed	2 500
		Balance c/d	18 500
	75 000		75 000
Jun 1 Balance b/d	18 500		

Apart from the actual figures, the entries in the Sales Ledger Control Account exactly reflect the entries in Mr Thompson's personal account. It will be easy to see from this why the totals of all debtors' balances carried down at the end of the month will be expected to equal the balance carried down on the Control Account.

Example 3.2. The following transactions relate to the credit sales of a firm which commenced business on 1 May. Record these transactions in the appropriate ledger accounts, extract a schedule of debtors as at 31 May and check the total debtors' figure against the balance of the Sales Ledger Control Account.

May 10 Credit sales: J. Brown: £200; H. Green: £300; B. White: £400
" 15 Credit sales: W. Black: £150; T. Pink: £100
" 21 J. Brown pays by cheque £190, discount allowed £10

Credit sales: B. Gold: £500; L. Silver: £80

" 31 H. Green and B. White pay the amounts owed by them
by cheque less 5% discount

Credit sales: J. Brown: £250

Solution

Cash Book (extract)

	Discount	Cash	Bank	
	£	£	£	£
May 21 J. Brown	10	–	190	
" 31 H. Green	15	–	285	
B. White	20	–	380	
	45		855	

Sales Ledger

J. Brown

	£		£
May 10 Sales	200	May 21 Bank	190
" 31 Sales	250	Discount	10
		Balance c/d	250
	450		450
Jun 1 Balance b/d	250		

H. Green

	£		£
May 10 Sales	300	May 31 Bank	285
		Discount	15
	300		300

B. White

	£		£
May 10 Sales	400	May 31 Bank	380
		Discount	20
	400		400

W. Black

	£		£
May 15 Sales	150		

T. Pink

	£	£
May 15 Sales	100	

B. Gold

	£	£
May 21 Sales	500	

I. Silver

	£	£
May 21 Sales	80	

General Ledger

Sales Account

	£			£
May 31 Balance c/d	1980	May 10	Sundry Debtors	900
		" 15	Sundry Debtors	250
		" 21	Sundry Debtors	580
		" 31	J. Brown	250
	1980			1980
		June 1	Balance b/d	1980

Discounts Allowed

	£	£
May 31 Sundry debtors	45	

Schedule of Debtors

	£
J. Brown	250
W. Black	150
T. Pink	100
B. Gold	500
I. Silver	80
	1080

Sales Ledger Control Account

	£		£
Sales	1980	Bank	855
		Discounts	45
		Balance c/d	1080
	1980		1980
Balance b/d	1080		

The total of the schedule of debtors equals the balance carried down on the Sales Ledger Control Account, from which we may assume that, numerically at any rate, the postings to the Sales Ledger are correct. It should also be noticed that the Control Account provides a quick and convenient way of arriving at the total of outstanding debtors – which can be useful, if this information is needed in a hurry.

This example has been kept as simple as possible, for the sake of clarity. In practice it would be necessary to take account of a number of other items affecting credit sales, such as returns inwards, dishonoured cheques and interest charged on overdue accounts.

Bank reconciliations

Just as Sales Ledger and Purchases Ledger entries are subject to checking by Control Accounts, so too the firm's Bank Account entries in the Cash Book can be verified by reference to statements provided periodically by the bank. By definition, the Bank Account records all the deposits into and withdrawals from the bank, so that, in theory, it should be possible at any time to show that the balance at the bank is in accordance with the balance in the 'Bank' column of the Cash Book. It is unlikely, in fact, that the balance shown in a statement of account issued by the bank will be identical with the balance carried down in the Cash Book, for a number of reasons:

(a) There will usually be cheques issued by the firm and entered in the Cash Book which have not yet been presented to the bank for payment. The bank statement will therefore show a *higher* balance than the Cash Book.

(b) The firm may have made a deposit on the day on which the bank statement was prepared, and this deposit may not be included in the bank statement. In this respect, the bank statement will show a *lower* balance than the Cash Book.

(c) The bank is often used for transactions – credit transfers or standing orders – which do not involve the payment or receipt of cheques and which would therefore not usually be recorded in the Cash Book until the bank statement is received. The same is true of interest or other items charged by the bank to the firm's account.

The process of checking will start by entering the items described in (c) above in the Cash Book and calculating an amended Cash Book balance. This amended balance will then be reconciled with the balance on the bank statement by (i) adding to it unpresented cheques and (ii) subtracting from it deposits not yet recorded by the bank.

Example 3.3. W. Cartwright's Cash Book showed a debit bank balance of £962 on 31 March. The statement from the bank showed that he had £1060 to the credit of his current account. His records reveal the following information:

(1) Cheques issued to D. Smith for £170 and S. Brown for £320 had not been presented for payment to the bank.
(2) A payment of £83 from T. Jones made direct to the bank by credit transfer had not been recorded in the Cash Book.
(3) A payment of £120 for motor insurance made by bank standing order had also not been recorded in the Cash Book.
(4) Bank charges for the month amounted to £15.
(5) A bank deposit of £340 made on the afternoon of 31 March had not been included in the bank statement.

Make the necessary entries in the Cash Book, then reconcile the corrected Cash Book balance with the balance shown in the bank statement.

Solution

Cash Book

	£		£
Balance b/d	962	Standing Order	
		– Insurance	120
Credit Transfer –		Bank Charges	15
T. Jones	83		
		Balance c/d	910
	1045		1045

Bank Reconciliation

	£	£
Corrected Cash Book balance		910
add: Unpresented cheques –		
D. Smith	170	
S. Brown	320	490
		1400
less: Unrecorded deposit		340
Balance as per bank statement		1060

Exercises

Exercise 3.1. On preparing a trial balance, a trader found that the debit balances exceeded the credit balances by £485. The following errors were subsequently discovered:

(a) Discount allowed of £13 had been correctly credited to P. Floyd's account, but no other entry had been made.

(b) A payment of £682 by D. Straits had been credited to the account of R. Stones.

(c) A total in the Sales Day Book of £321 had been carried forward to the next page as £231.

(d) The debit side of the Rent Account had been overcast by £300.

(e) £3000 spent on materials for the building of extensions to the firm's premises had been debited to the Purchases Account.

(f) A payment of £108 by B. Rats had been recorded in the Cash Book but not posted to the Sales Ledger.

Show the necessary correcting entries in the Journal and in the Suspense Account.

Exercise 3.2. A firm's books showed the following Sales Ledger and Purchases Ledger transactions for the year, its first trading period:

	£
Sales	75300
Purchases	51500
Cash from credit customers	69520

Cash paid to creditors	47100
Sales returns	400
Purchases returns	250
Discounts allowed	1560
Discounts received	910

Prepare the Sales Ledger Control Account and the Purchases Ledger Control Account. What conclusions can be drawn from the fact that the total balances extracted from the Sales ledger and Purchases ledger were £3820 (Dr) and £2940 (Cr) respectively at the end of the year?

Exercise 3.3. A trader's Cash Book showed a debit balance of £561 on 31 December. His bank balance on the same date, as indicated by the statement from his bank, was £789 (Cr). He ascertains from his records that:

(a) A payment of £200 from B. Little made direct to his bank had not been recorded in the Cash Book.

(b) Cheques issued to F. Widgeon and O. Prosser for £125 and £270 respectively had not been presented.

(c) A cheque from S. Ukridge for £85 had been dishonoured. (Hint: Mr Ukridge's personal account is debited to reverse the credit entry made at the time his cheque was received. What does this tell us about the entry that must be made in the 'Bank' columns of the Cash Book?)

(d) Bank charges amounting to £23 had not been recorded in the Cash Book.

(e) A bank deposit of £109 did not appear on the bank statement.

(f) A payment of £150 had been made by the bank in terms of a standing order to the Mulliner Fire Insurance Society.

Record the necessary additional entries in the Cash Book, then reconcile the amended Cash Book balance with the bank statement.

2 The Reporting Function

4 Reporting Trading Results: Gross Profit

The purpose of recording information

We have seen that one reason for recording information is the need to ascertain and define the firm's rights and obligations. It is necessary to know the precise value of the owner's investment in the business, how much money is owed to the firm by debtors and how much is due to creditors. But none of these rights and obligations would have arisen if it had not been for the owner's motive in the first place: to make a profit. The recording system must also therefore be designed in such a way as to enable the recorded information to be brought together in report form to disclose the results of trading.

The determination of profit for any particular period requires two distinct operations. It is necessary, first, to deduct the cost of purchasing the goods sold from the income derived from their sale; this is done by means of the **Trading Account**, which indicates the **gross profit** – or, of course, *gross loss* – for the period. This gross profit must then be adjusted to take account of expenses, other than the cost of purchasing the goods, incurred by the firm during the period. This is the function of the **Profit and Loss Account**, which shows the **net profit**, or *net loss*, accruing to the business.

A.—4

The Trading Account

Take the case of a retail shopkeeper, R. Green, who has drawn up a trial balance at 31 December 1985 which discloses the following information:

	Dr	Cr
	£	£
Capital		10000
Bank	5600	
Cash	300	
Vehicles	3000	
Stock at 1 January 1985	2000	
Purchases	15000	
Sales		24200
Returns Inwards	200	
Returns Outwards		100
Discounts Allowed	300	
Discounts Received		150
Debtors	6000	
Creditors		4750
Wages	3000	
Rent	1500	
Electricity	2300	
	39200	39200

From these balances we have first to separate out those items which relate strictly to the *cost of goods sold* and to the *income received from them*. To arrive at the cost of goods sold we need to know:

(a) the value of any goods purchased during the previous year which had not been sold before the first day of the current year (these goods, which are shown in the trial balance as 'Stock at 1 January 1985', would obviously have been available for sale during 1985);

(b) the value of goods purchased during the course of the year, less any goods returned to suppliers; and

(c) the value of any goods *unsold* at the end of the year. (This figure, known as *closing stock*, does not appear in the trial balance because it can be ascertained only by physically checking the goods in the firm's store-room or warehouse on the last day of the year. Let us assume that in this case it was valued at £5900.)

Once we have arrived at the cost of goods sold, we deduct it from
the *net sales* for the period, that is, from the sales figure after it has
been adjusted for *returns inwards* from customers. We have now
established the gross profit for the year.

Trading Account of R. Green
for the year ending 31 December 1985

	£	£	£
Sales		24200	
less: Returns Inwards		200	24000
Cost of goods sold:			
Opening Stock		2000	
Purchases	15000		
less: Returns Outwards	100	14900	
		16900	
less: Closing Stock		5900	
			11000
Gross profit			13000

Stock valuation

While it is a simple matter to ascertain the value of purchases for the year – since this merely involves calculating the
balance to be carried to the Trading Account from the Purchases
Account – the value of the closing stock (which is, of course, the
value of the opening stock for the *following year*) does present difficulties. Not only is a physical check necessary to establish the *quantity* of goods remaining; the problem then arises of deciding what
value to attach to this quantity. If the prices of all goods purchased
remained uniformly stable throughout the year, there would be no
difficulty; however, as things are, allowance has to be made for fluc-
tuating prices. Suppose, for the sake of simplicity, that Mr Green
retailed only one type of article and that his opening stock on 1
January consisted of 250 articles valued at £8 each. Let us also
suppose that his purchases and sales for the year were:

	Purchases	£	Sales	£
January	375@£8	= 3000	100@£20 =	2000
March	400@£10	= 4000	–	–
April	–	–	600@£20 =	12000
June	250@£12	= 3000	–	–
September	400@£12.50	= 5000	500@£20 =	10000
	1425	15000	1200	24000

If Mr Green started the year with 250 articles and then purchased a further 1425, he must have had a total of 1675 articles available for sale. If 1200 of these were sold, then 475 must have remained unsold. How is Mr Green to value this closing stock? Even if it were possible, there would be no point in his trying to recollect from which batch of purchases each remaining article derived, since all the articles are physically identical. What he will actually do is select one of the three accepted bases of valuation:

(a) First In, First Out (or FIFO)
(b) Last In, First Out (or LIFO)
(c) Average Cost (or AVCO)

(a) *First In, First Out*

This method assumes that goods taken out of stock were issued from those articles which were received *earliest*. Thus the 600 articles sold in April are assumed to be made up as follows: 150 articles at £8 taken from the opening stock (the other 100 articles from opening stock had been sold in January); plus 375 articles at £8 bought in January; plus 75 articles at £10 bought in March.

Date	Purchases	Sales		Balance of stock	
Opening stock	–	–		250 × £8	= £2000
January	375 × £8	100		525 × £8	= £4200
March	400 × £10	–		525 × £8	
			plus	400 × £10	= £8200
April	–	600		325 × £10	= £3250
June	250 × £12	–		325 × £10	
			plus	250 × £12	= £6250
September	400 × £12.50	500		75 × £12	
			plus	400 × £12.50	= £5900

Since there were no further purchases or sales between September and the end of the year, the closing stock value is taken as £5 900, which is the figure appearing in Mr Green's Trading Account.

(b) Last In, First Out

The LIFO method makes a directly opposite assumption – that goods are issued from the stock *most recently* received. On this basis, Mr Green's closing stock would have been valued at £4 400.

(c) Average Cost

The AVCO method arrives at the valuation by adding the total value of goods received to the total value of the stock already in hand and then dividing the sum of these two figures by the total number of articles, thus establishing an average cost for each article.

Date	Purchases	Average cost	Sales	Balance of stock	
Opening stock	–	–	–	250 × £8	= £2 000
January	375 × £8	£8	100	525 × £8	= £4 200
March	400 × £10	£8.87	–	925 × £8.87	= £8 200
April	–	£8.87	600	325 × £8.87	= £2 883
June	250 × £12	£10.23	–	575 × £10.23	= £5 883
September	400 × £12.50	£11.16	500	475 × £11.16	= £5 302

The average cost of the goods in stock at the end of March is calculated as follows:

Goods in stock at 31 January (525 × £8)	= £4 200
Goods purchased in March (400 × £10)	= £4 000
Total cost of goods now in stock	£8 200

Total number of articles now in stock: 925

Therefore average cost of each article: £8 200 ÷ 925 = £8.87

The 600 articles sold in April are therefore taken as having cost £8.87 each, and the balance remaining at the end of April is calculated as 325 × £8.87 = £2 883.

During inflationary periods the FIFO method will always give the

highest value for closing stock and the LIFO method the lowest,
with the AVCO method coming between the two. This is an important consideration, because the value chosen for the closing stock
can make a substantial difference to the profit reported for the year,
as can be seen by examining the effect of each method on Mr Green's
Trading Account:

Method	Value of closing stock	Gross profit
FIFO	£5900	£13000
LIFO	£4400	£11500
AVCO	£5302	£12402

However, because the *closing stock* for this year is the *opening stock*
for next year, profits will tend to equalize over a number of years
regardless of which method is chosen – provided, of course, that the
accounting **convention of consistency** is observed and the method
of valuation is not changed arbitrarily from year to year.

One further thing remains to be said about stock valuation. If the
firm knows that the **realizable value** of stock on hand – that is, the
amount which would be received if the stock were sold at current
market prices – is *lower* than the cost indicated by the FIFO, LIFO
or AVCO methods, then it must value its closing stock at this lower,
or realizable, value rather than at cost. This is in accordance with
the accounting **convention of prudence** (or **conservatism**) which
requires accountants to take every possible precaution against over-
stating profit.

The Manufacturing Account

The Trading Account we have been discussing is the
appropriate means of determining the gross profit of a *retailer*, that
is, a trader who purchases the goods he intends to re-sell. In the case
of a *manufacturer*, something more is needed, since the cost of goods
manufactured for sale contains a number of different elements, each
of which must be ascertained and accounted for. The Manufacturing
Account analyses and collates these elements under two main head-

ings: **prime cost** and **overheads**. The distinction between these two categories is an important one, for reasons which will be explained in Chapter 9. In the present context, it is sufficient to know that prime cost is the total *variable cost* of production, that is, that part of the total cost which *varies directly* with the volume of production, while the term overheads covers all other manufacturing costs.

Let us assume that Mr B. Jones has incurred the following manufacturing costs over the course of a year:

	£
Purchases of raw materials	150000
Wages paid to factory workers	60000
Supervisory wages	14000
Electricity	24000
Factory rent	12000
Machinery maintenance	17000

Let us also suppose that his accounts disclosed the following opening and closing stock balances:

	£
Opening stock of raw materials	8000
Opening stock of work-in-progress (work commenced but not completed in the *previous* year)	5000
Closing stock of raw materials	7000
Closing stock of work-in-progress (work commenced but not completed in the *current* year)	4000

Manufacturing Account

	£	£
Raw materials:		
Opening stock		8000
Purchases		150000
		158000
less: Closing stock		7000
Cost of materials used		151000
Wages		60000
Prime cost		211000

Overheads:

Supervisory wages	14000	
Electricity	24000	
Factory rent	12000	
Machine maintenance	17000	67000
		278000
add: Opening stock of work-in-progress		5000
		283000
less: Closing stock of work-in-progress		4000
Cost of goods produced (to Trading Account)		279000

Example 4.1.   A manufacturer's trial balance at 31 December 1985 revealed the following information:

	Dr	Cr
	£	£
Capital		200000
Bank	5600	
Cash	500	
Premises	90000	
Machinery	40000	
Vehicles	35000	
Stock of raw materials at 1 January 1985	4000	
Stock of finished goods at 1 January 1985	6000	
Direct factory wages	50000	
Factory supervision	7000	
Electricity:Factory	12000	
Office	4000	
Machinery maintenance	2500	
General factory expenses	2000	
Office salaries	6000	
General administration expenses	22000	
Sales		193300
Work-in-progress at 1 January 1985	5400	
Purchases of raw materials	70000	
Purchases Returns		1200
Sales Returns	2500	
Debtors	30000	
	394500	394500

Notes

(1) Closing stock balances were: Raw materials   £6000

Finished goods   £8000

Work-in-progress   £4000

(2) One major item of raw materials had been charged out on

a LIFO basis. An adjustment is necessary to correct this to a FIFO valuation. Purchases and issues of this item were:

Date	Purchases	Issues
April	3000 @ £4	–
May	2000 @ £4.25	3500
August	3000 @ £5.00	4000
October	1000 @ £5.50	500

You are required to construct the Manufacturing and Trading Accounts and determine the gross profit.

Solution The first step is to effect the adjustment to the closing stock of raw materials required by Note 2.

Date	Purchases	Issues	Balance	
LIFO			–	£
April	3000 × 4	–	3000 × 4	= 12000
May	2000 × 4.25	2000 × 4.25		
		1500 × 4.00	1500 × 4	= 6000
August	3000 × 5	3000 × 5.00		
		1000 × 4.00	500 × 4	= 2000
October	1000 × 5.50	500 × 5.50	500 × 5.50	
			500 × 4.00	= 4750
FIFO				
April	3000 × 4	–	3000 × 4	= 12000
May	2000 × 4.25	3000 × 4		
		500 × 4.25	1500 × 4.25	= 6375
August	3000 × 5	1500 × 4.25		
		2500 × 5.00	500 × 5	= 2500
October	1000 × 5.50	500 × 5.00	1000 × 5.50	= 5500

The closing stock of raw materials must therefore be increased by £750 (that is, £5500 – £4750).

Manufacturing Account

	£	£
Opening stock of raw materials		4000
add: Purchases	70000	
less: Returns	1200	68800
		72800
less: Closing stock (£6000 + £750)		6750
Cost of materials consumed		66050
Direct wages		50000
Prime cost		116050

Overheads:

Supervision	7000	
Electricity	12000	
Machinery maintenance	2500	
General expenses	2000	23500
		139550
add: Work-in-progress 1 January		5400
		144950
less: Work-in-progress 31 December		4000
Cost of goods produced		140950

Trading Account

	£	£	£
Sales		193300	
less: Returns		2500	190800
Opening stock of finished goods	6000		
add: Cost of goods produced	140950		
	146950		
less: Stock of finished goods	8000		138950
Gross profit			51850

Exercises

Exercise 4.1.   A firm's purchases and sales of a particular item during the course of a year were as follows:

	Purchases	*Sales*	
March	500 @ £8 each	April	300
June	400 @ £10 each	July	400
August	300 @ £12 each	September	300

(There was no stock on hand at the beginning of the year.)

You are required to value the stock in hand at the end of the year according to the (1) First In, First Out, (2) Last In, First Out, and (3) Average Cost methods, and to calculate the gross profit on each of these methods, if the goods were sold at a unit selling price of £15.

Exercise 4.2.   Prepare Manufacturing and Trading Accounts from the following balances of Artoo Limited, a manufacturer of robots, for the year ended 30 June 1985:

	£
Stocks at 1 July 1984:	
Raw materials	28 450
Work-in-progress	3 360
Finished goods	20 500
Purchases: raw materials	78 600
Direct labour	61 200
Factory fuel and power	8 300
Rent	3 600
Sales	250 100

Notes

(1) Of the Rent expense, two-thirds relates to the factory.

(2) Stocks at 30 June 1985 were:

Raw materials	£23 210
Work-in-progress	£1 840
Finished goods	£17 800

5 Reporting Trading Results: Net Profit

The Profit and Loss Account

Every business concern engaged in buying and selling goods will incur expenses other than those connected with the purchase of articles for sale; these expenses must be accounted for before the revenue from sales can be regarded as properly due to the owner, or owners, of the firm. They will in most cases have been paid and the payments by cash or cheque will have resulted in debit balances appearing in the trial balance.

From the trial balance for Mr R. Green which appeared in Chapter 4, we were able to calculate Mr Green's gross profit as £13 000. To arrive at his net profit for the year, we must adjust this figure by deducting the balances for wages, rent and electricity.

Trading and Profit and Loss Account of R. Green for the year ending 31 December 1985

	£	£	£
Sales		24 200	
less: Returns Inwards		200	24 000
Cost of goods sold:			
Opening stock		2 000	
Purchases	15 000		
less: Returns Outwards	100	14 900	
		16 900	
less: Closing stock		5 900	11 000
Gross profit			13 000
Expenses:			
Wages		3 000	
Rent		1 500	
Electricity		2 300	6 800
Net profit			6 200

Accruals and prepayments

In terms of the **accruals concept** of accounting, all
expenses due for the year – whether paid or not – must be deducted
from all the *revenue due* for the year – whether received or not –
before the net profit can be regarded as properly calculated. If this
principle is ignored, it will be impossible to make the necessary
distinction between a firm's profit and its *cash flow*. It will rarely be
possible for a firm to ensure that all its expenses have been paid for
the year by the date on which the final accounts are drawn up. Local
authorities and utilities often dispatch statements of account after
the end of the financial year, and these statements will almost always
show amounts due in arrear, or in advance. Insurance payments are
always payable in advance, which means that all annual payments,
unless made on the first day of the financial year, will include an
element of prepayment for the following year.

In the case of Mr Green's accounts, let us say that the following
adjustments are necessary:

   (a) Wages of £200 are due to an employee who was absent
       from work on the last day of the month.
   (b) The rent payment included an amount of £300 paid in
       advance for the quarter ending 31 March 1986.

Two adjustments are therefore necessary, one to take account of
accrued wages, the other to exclude from the current year's expenses
the rent *prepaid* for the following year. These adjustments will be
made in Mr Green's Profit and Loss Account as follows:

	£	£	£
Gross Profit			13000
Expenses:			
Wages	3000		
add: accrued	200	3200	
Rent	1500		
less: prepaid	300	1200	
Electricity		2300	6700
Net profit			6300

Depreciation of assets

The expenses we have been examining are easily ascertainable; they are either payments which have already been made or expenses which we know to have been prepaid or to be still due for payment. There are other profit and loss items which are equally necessary but which cannot always be obtained from the trial balance. The most important of these is the expense implied by the term 'depreciation'.

Just as wages paid to sales staff are an expense which must be recouped out of sales revenue before profit can be determined, so also is the cost of a motor van acquired for the purpose of delivering goods to customers. The main difference between the two expenses is this: the wage payment is, allowing for minor adjustments for accruals and prepayments, a payment made specifically for the year and is therefore an obvious charge to the current Profit and Loss Account; the cost of a van, however – a *fixed asset* – is properly chargeable as an expense not only in the year when it is bought but in all the years during which it benefits the firm.

There are a number of ways in which this depreciation can be effected. The following are among the most important:

(a) *The straight line or fixed instalment method*

This method assumes that the usefulness of the asset is approximately equal in each year of its life-span. Thus, if a motor van costs £20000 and is expected to last five years, it will be *depreciated* at one-fifth of its value each year; that is, £4000 will be charged to the Profit and Loss Account each year over five successive years. A journal transfer is made, debiting the Profit and Loss Account and crediting a special Provision for Depreciation on Motor Vans Account. Note that no actual payment – beyond the original payment for the asset at the time that it was bought – is involved; the effect of the journal transfer is to retain each year within the firm £4000 which would otherwise be treated as profit at the disposal of the owner of the firm.

Provision for Depreciation on Motor Vans

	£		£
Year 1 Balance c/d	4000	Year 1 Profit and Loss	4000
Year 2 Balance c/d	8000	Year 2 Balance b/d	4000
		Profit and Loss	4000
	8000		8000
		Year 3 Balance b/d	8000

(b) The reducing balance method

Some firms prefer to match the expense of depreciation more precisely against the benefit received from the asset, on the principle
that the service given by the asset is most valuable when it is new
and becomes progressively less valuable as it grows older. They
therefore use one or other variant of what is known as the 'reducing
balance method'. In its simplest form, this involves calculating the
depreciation at a predetermined rate, not on the original cost but on
the *depreciated value* at the end of the previous accounting period.
In the example already given, assuming an annual rate of 20%, the
charge against Profit and Loss Account would be £4000 for the first
year, exactly as with the straight line method, but for the second
year it would be 20% of (£20000 – £4000), and in the third year 20% of
(£20000 – £4000 – £3200).

Provision for Depreciation on Motor Vans

	£		£
Year 1 Balance c/d	4000	Year 1 Profit and Loss	4000
Year 2 Balance c/d	7200	Year 2 Balance b/d	4000
		Profit and Loss	3200
	7200		7200
Year 3 Balance c/d	9760	Year 3 Balance b/d	7200
		Profit and Loss	2560
	9760		9760
		Year 4 Balance b/d	9760

(c) The revaluation method

The methods we have been discussing are not suitable for calculating depreciation on certain types of asset, particularly those composed of a large number of discrete items, such as livestock or workshop tools. In these cases, the procedure normally adopted is to value the asset as accurately as possible each year and then treat the difference between each year and the next as depreciation for that year. If a firm purchases tools valued at £4000 on 1 January of Year 1 and the values at the end of each successive year are: Year 1, £3500; Year 2, £3200; Year 3, £2800, then:

Provision for Depreciation on Loose Tools

		£			£
Year 1	Balance c/d	500	Year 1	Profit and Loss	500
Year 2	Balance c/d	800	Year 2	Balance b/d	500
				Profit and Loss	300
		800			800
Year 3	Balance c/d	1200	Year 3	Balance b/d	800
				Profit and Loss	400
		1200			1200
			Year 4	Balance b/d	1200

It should be noted that, while all these methods do recover the original cost of the asset from the revenue provided by sales, they do not automatically provide for the replacement of the asset when its useful life is over. The money retained from distribution as profit will quite certainly be spent in the ordinary course of business expenditure on purchases, wages and other expense items unless steps are taken to invest an annual amount of cash equivalent to the profit and loss charge for the year in an external investment which will mature at the time when the asset is due to be scrapped. This is what is known as a **Sinking Fund**. Because the interest earned each year is re-invested and therefore compounded, both the expense charged to the Profit and Loss Account and the cash invested each year will be less than the depreciation which would be charged without a Sinking Fund.

Assets are frequently disposed of before the anticipated end of their useful life. This can happen for a number of reasons, the sale of the asset because it has become technologically out of date, say, or its destruction by accident. What is done in these cases is to transfer the original cost of the asset, by journal, to the debit of a **Disposals Account**. This account is then credited with both (i) the proceeds of the sale of the asset and (ii) the amount so far accumulated as depreciation on the asset. The balance on the Disposals Account will then represent a profit or loss on disposal which must be credited (if a profit) or debited (if a loss) to the Profit and Loss Account.

Suppose that a motor van, purchased on 1 January 1981 for £20000 and which was being depreciated at 20% on the straight line method, was involved in a serious accident and had to be scrapped on 1 January 1984, and that an insurance payment of £3000 was subsequently received. The following journal and ledger entries would be required in 1984 (assuming that the firm possessed no other motor vans).

Journal

	Dr	Cr
	£	£
(a) Disposals Account	20000	
Motor Van		20000
Transfer of value of asset to Disposals Account		
(b) Bank	3000	
Disposals Account		3000
Cheque received from insurance company		
(c) Provision for Depreciation on Motor Van	12000	
Disposals Account		12000
Transfer of accumulated provision on motor van		
(d) Profit and Loss	5000	
Disposals Account		5000
Loss on disposal of van		

General Ledger

Motor Van

		£			£
1984			1984		
Jan 1 Balance b/d		20000	Jan 1 Disposals		20000

A.—5

Provision for Depreciation on Motor Van

		£			£
1984			1984		
Jan 1 Disposals		12000	Jan 1 Balance b/d		12000

Disposals Account

	£		£
1984		1984	
Jan 1 Motor Van	20000	Jan 1 Provision for	
		Depreciation	12000
		Bank	3000
		Profit and Loss	5000
	20000		20000

The logic of the transfer from the Provision for Depreciation to the Disposals Account may not be immediately apparent. It is necessary for two reasons. First, the asset has been disposed of and it is no longer necessary to maintain a provision account for it. Second, a certain amount of the original cost has been recovered from revenue by the ordinary process of depreciation, and this has been supplemented by the payment received on disposal; this may not equal the full original cost, and any shortfall will have to be recovered by a special debit to the Profit and Loss Account. The transfer of depreciation to the Disposals Account enables this adjustment to be made.

Bad debts

One of the risks of business to which every firm is exposed is that money due for goods sold on credit will not be paid. Most firms attach great importance to careful credit management; but even in the most favourable circumstances there will be customers who will not, or cannot, pay their debts. The revenue lost in this way must be taken into account when calculating net profit.

Suppose that Mr J. Smith who bought goods worth £400 in May is declared bankrupt in September without having paid his debt. There is no point in maintaining an open account indefinitely if it is certain, or almost certain, that payment will not be made, so the firm will sooner or later, but preferably within the current accounting year, 'write off' the debt as bad. This is done by means of the following entries:

Journal

	Dr	Cr
	£	£
(a) Bad Debts	400	
J. Smith		400
Bad debt written off		
(b) Profit and Loss	400	
Bad Debts		400
Bad debts charged to Profit and Loss		

J. Smith

	£		£
Sep 30 Balance b/d	400	Sep 30 Bad Debts	400

Bad Debts

	£		£
Sep 30 J. Smith	400	Dec 31 Profit and Loss	400

Profit and Loss (extract)

	£		£
Bad Debts	£400		

(It is assumed in this example that there is only one debt written off as bad during the course of the year.)

Unfortunately, it cannot be assumed that, because all debts known to be bad have been written off, the firm's losses from this source have been fully accounted for. A number of other debts will remain *doubtful*. Firms will know from their experience of past years that at the end of the year a certain percentage of current debts will not have been paid. If no adjustment is made for this probable loss in the current year's final account, then it will be carried forward to the following year and set off as an expense against that year's sales – which, of course, is not in accordance with the accruals concept. If the firm's experience is that 3% on average of its debtors at the end of the year – after having written off known bad debts – do not pay what they owe, the firm will charge this amount to its Profit and Loss Account as an expense and credit a **Provision for Doubtful Debts**

Account. If in the case we have been considering the debtor balances totalled £20000 after writing off J. Smith's bad debt, then £600 (that is 3% of £20000) will be charged to Profit and Loss and credited to the provision. The balance on the provision is carried down to the following year and then adjusted at the end of that year so that it becomes equal to the new provision required. If in this example the following year's final debtor total – again after writing off known bad debts – amounts to £25000, the transfer to the provision from Profit and Loss will be £150, i.e. the new provision now required: £750 (3% of £25000), *less* the £600 brought forward from the previous year.

Provision for Doubtful Debts

	£			£
Year 1 Balance c/d	600	Year 1 Profit and Loss		600
Year 2		Year 2		
Dec 31 Balance c/d	750	Jan 1 Balance b/d		600
		Dec 31 Profit and Loss		150
	750			750
		Year 3		
		Jan 1 Balance b/d		750

Discounts

Not all of the income appearing as net sales in the Trading Account will actually be received because many customers will take advantage of the discount terms offered by the firm. Further adjustments are therefore required to take advantage of both (i) discounts allowed during the course of the year and (ii) discounts which will be deducted from payments due to be made by customers owing money at the end of the year.

The first of these adjustments is straightforward. From our discussion on the Cash Book in Chapter 2 it will be recalled that the Cash Book is debited with discount allowed to customers and that customers' personal accounts are credited. The total of the Discounts Allowed column in the Cash Book is then posted to the debit of the Discounts Allowed Account. In a case where a firm had allowed discounts up to 1 December to the amount of £250 and then allowed a further £50 discount during December, the transfers would show:

Discount Allowed

		£			£
Dec 1	Balance b/d	250	Dec 31	Profit and Loss	300
Dec 31	Cash Book –				
	Sundry debtors	50			
		300			300

Journal

	Dr	Cr
	£	£
Profit and Loss	300	
Discounts Allowed		300
Discounts Allowed charged to Profit and Loss		

Profit and Loss Account (extract)

	£		£
Discounts Allowed	300		

A similar adjustment must of course be made for the *discounts received* from the firm's creditors as these discounts will *increase* the firm's reported profit.

Discounts Received

		£			£
Dec 31	Profit and Loss	150	Dec 1	Balance b/d (say)	125
			Dec 31	Cash Book –	
				Sundry creditors	25
		150			150

Journal

	Dr	Cr
	£	£
Discounts Received	150	
Profit and Loss		150
Discounts Received credited to Profit and Loss		

Profit and Loss (extract)

	£		£
		Discounts Received	150

The adjustment for discounts allowed to current debtors is rather less simple, and here again the firm must be guided by its past experience. If the firm has come to expect that about 2% of debtors outstanding at 31 December will pay their debts within the period stipulated for discount, then it must allow for a corresponding reduction in the sales income for the year. As in the case of doubtful debts, the Profit and Loss Account is debited and a provision account is credited. On our assumption that current year-end debtors are £20000 as above and that our Provision for Doubtful Debts is £600, the **Provision for Discounts Allowed** will be 2% of (£20000−£600), or £388. (The reason for deducting the Provision for Doubtful Debts from the debtors' total is that there is no point in allowing for discount on debts which are probably not going to be paid.) The balance on the Provision for Discounts Allowed Account is carried down and adjusted in the following year in precisely the same way as the balance on the Provision for Doubtful Debts Account. Thus, making the same assumption on Year 2 as above:

Provision for Discounts Allowed					
		£			£
Year 1			Year 1		
Dec 31	Balance c/d	388	Dec 31	Profit and Loss	388
Year 2			Year 2		
Dec 31	Balance c/d	485	Jan 1	Balance b/d	388
			Dec 31	Profit and Loss	97
		485			485
			Year 3		
			Jan 1	Balance b/d	485

The calculation of the Profit and Loss charge for Year 2 is as follows:

Required new provision: 2% of (£25000 − £750)   = £485
less: Balance brought down from Year 1   = £388
Charge to Profit and Loss Account   = £ 97

Example 5.1. The following trial balance was extracted from the accounts of S. Thompson, a grocer, on 31 December 1985.

	Dr	Cr
	£	£
Sales		65 000
Purchases	47 000	
Sales Returns	1 500	
Purchases Returns		2 250
Stock 1 January 1985	7 000	

Drawings	12 000	
Bad debts written off	550	
Provision for doubtful debts		720
Wages and salaries	8 000	
Shop fittings	12 000	
Vehicles, at cost	30 000	
Debtors	18 000	
Creditors		11 000
Provision for discounts		280
Provision for depreciation:		
Vehicles		18 000
Shop fittings		2 400
Suspense Account		4 000
Discounts Allowed and		
Received	900	350
General expenses	5 270	
Capital		48 000
Cash at bank	9 500	
Cash in hand	280	
	152 000	152 000

Notes
(1) Stock at 31 December 1985 was £6 000.
(2) Wages accrued at 31 December 1985: £800.
 General Expenses prepaid at 31 December 1985: £490.
(3) The Provision for Doubtful Debts is maintained at 5%, the Provision for Discounts at 2%.
(4) A van bought in 1982 for £15 000 was disposed of on 20 December 1985 for £4 000 and this amount was posted to the Suspense Account, pending transfer to the correct account. The firm's policy is to depreciate all vehicles on hand at the end of each year by 20% on cost and to provide no depreciation in the year of sale.
(5) Shop fittings are to be depreciated at 10% on book value.

Prepare Mr Thompson's Trading and Profit and Loss Accounts.

Solution   Before proceeding to the construction of the Trading and Profit and Loss Accounts, it is necessary to calculate the adjustments which are required by the Notes.

Workings
   Note (2)   Wages accrued will increase the expense item for this year and must therefore be added. General expenses prepaid reflect a payment made for the following year and must therefore be subtracted to arrive at the general expenses for the year.
   Note (3)   The Provision for Doubtful Debts at the beginning of the year was £720. This must be increased by £180 to equal 5% of debtors, that is 5/100 × £18 000 = £900. The Profit and Loss Account is therefore

charged £180. The Provision for Discounts Allowed was £280 at the beginning of the year. This must be increased by £62 to equal 2% of debtors *after* providing for doubtful debts, that is 2/100 × (£18 000 − £900) = £342.

Note (4)   Since the van was bought in 1982, depreciation at 20% of cost will have been provided for it for 1982, 1983 and 1984, that is 20/100 × £15 000 × 3 = £9 000. This amount must be transferred from the Provision for Depreciation on Vehicles to the Disposals Account, which must also be credited with the £4 000 originally entered to the Suspense Account. The original value of the asset must of course be credited to the Vehicles Account and debited to the Disposals Account.

Disposals Account

	£		£
Vehicles	15 000	Provision for Depreciation	9 000
		Suspense Account	4 000
		Profit and Loss	2 000
	15 000		15 000

The loss on disposal, £2 000, is debited to the Profit and Loss Account. Depreciation must also be provided for on the remaining vehicles for the current year. This will be 20/100 × (£30 000 − £15 000) = £3 000.

Note (5)   Depreciation at 10% must be provided on the book value of Shop Fittings, that is – using the reducing balance method – 10/100 × (£12 000 − £2 400) = £960.

**Trading and Profit and Loss Account of S. Thompson
for Year ending 31 December 1985**

	£	£	£
Sales			65 000
less: Returns			1 500
			63 500
Opening stock		7 000	
Purchases	47 000		
less: Returns	2 250	44 750	
		51 750	
less: Closing stock		6 000	45 750
Gross profit			17 750
Discounts Received			350
			18 100

Wages	8000	
add: Accrued	800	8800
General expenses	5270	
less: Prepaid	490	4780
Discounts Allowed		900
Provision for Discounts		62
Bad debts written off		550
Provision for doubtful debts		180
Loss on disposal of van		2000
Depreciation on: Vehicles		3000
Shop fittings		960	21232
Net loss		3132

Mr Thompson's costs and expenses for the year have exceeded his revenue, and he has therefore incurred a net loss.

Exercises

Exercise 5.1.   From the following balances extracted from the books of a trader after his Trading Account had been completed, prepare a Profit and Loss Account for the year ended 31 December 1985:

	Dr	Cr
	£	£
Gross profit		45000
Office salaries	12000	
General expenses	9000	
Discounts Allowed and		
Received	650	800
Provision for Doubtful Debts		300
Debtors and Creditors	9000	7000
Insurance	600	
Premises	60000	
Bad debts	400	
Vehicles	8000	
Provision for Depreciation on		
Vehicles		2000
Stock 31 December 1985	4000	
Bank	2500	
Cash	800	
Drawings	3000	
Capital		34850
Loan		20000
	109950	109950

Notes
(1) Depreciation is to be provided at 10% on the cost of vehicles.
(2) The Provision for Doubtful Debts is to be adjusted to 5% of debtors.

(3) The insurance payment is for the year ending 31 March 1986.
(4) A payment of £300 is due on general expenses.

Exercise 5.2.   On 1 April 1982 a firm which had just commenced business purchased two machines for £12 000 and £8000. These machines were expected to have a useful life of five years and the amount to be provided for depreciation each year was determined on this basis. On 1 July 1985 the machine which had been bought for £8000 was sold for £1500. Calculate (1) the profit or loss on the sale of the asset, and (2) the balance carried down in the Provision for Depreciation Account on 31 March 1986.

6 The Balance Sheet

The purpose of the balance sheet

The **Balance Sheet** is the final stage in the reporting on a firm's transactions for the year. It assembles the balances remaining in the trial balance after the compilation of the Trading and Profit and Loss Account into a statement which lists (a) the **capital** and **liabilities** of the firm (that is, the money invested in the firm after taking account of profit for the year and money owed by the firm to external creditors); and (b) the uses, in the way of **fixed** and **current assets,** to which this money is being put. It is therefore a report on the financial condition of the firm at the end of the year. The manner in which it is presented will depend on the structure of the firm, that is to say, on whether ownership is vested in (1) a sole trader, (2) a partnership, or (3) a limited liability company.

The balance sheet of a sole trader

Let us suppose that A. Simpson's Profit and Loss Account for the year has disclosed a net profit of £15 000 and that the following balances remain open in his books:

	Dr	Cr
	£	£
Capital		80 000
Machinery	50 000	
Fixtures and fittings	20 000	
Vehicles	25 000	
Stock	20 000	
Debtors	6 000	
Bank	8 000	
Cash in hand	500	
Provisions for Depreciation:		
Machinery		8 000

Fixtures		2 000
Vehicles		6 000
Drawings	12 000	
Provision for Doubtful Debts		300
Provision for Discounts Allowed		114
Rent (owing)		170
Insurance (prepaid)	84	
Loan – A. Green		20 000
Creditors		10 000

Mr Simpson's Capital Account balance stood at £80 000 at the beginning of the year, and this was the value of his investment as at that date. Since then, the firm has made a profit of £15 000, all of which accrues to him as sole owner. On the other hand, he has drawn £12 000 out of the firm, as shown by the debit balance on his Drawings Account. The value of his investment at the end of the year therefore stands at (£80 000 + £15 000 − £12 000), or £83 000. This will make up the capital element in his balance sheet. The liabilities section will list debts owed to persons outside the firm, that is **long-term liabilities** (in this case the loan from Mr Green of £20 000), and **current liabilities** or amounts due to creditors for goods purchased (£10 000) and the unpaid rent due to the owner of the premises (£170).

**Balance Sheet of A. Simpson
as at 31 December 1985**

	£	£
Capital and liabilities		
Capital at 1 January	80 000	
add: Profit	15 000	
	95 000	
less: Drawings	12 000	83 000
Long-term liability		
Loan – A. Green		20 000
Current liabilities		
Trade creditors	10 000	
Expense creditors (Rent)	170	10 170
		113 170

The **assets** section of the balance sheet distinguishes between **fixed assets**, which do not form part of the trading transactions of the firm and which remain relatively unchanged throughout the year, and **current assets** which are directly affected by the process of trade and are in a state of constant change. Within this classification, the

individual asset items are themselves ranked in the order of their
relative *permanence*. In Mr Simpson's trial balance, machinery
would be regarded as the most permanent of the assets and would
therefore appear as the first item in his fixed assets, followed by
fixtures and fittings and then by vehicles. Each of these assets must
be shown at its current value, that is at its original cost less the
amount provided for depreciation. Among the current assets, stock
changes least quickly and is therefore ranked first, followed by
debtors, bank and cash. The debtor item must, however, be shown
at a value which takes account of the adjustments provided in the
Profit and Loss Account for Doubtful Debts and Discounts Allowed.
It is also necessary to take account of expenses paid in advance – in
this case the insurance prepaid (£84) – on the principle that money
paid in advance remains the property of the firm until it is legally
due for payment and is, therefore, 'owed', for the moment, by the
payee.

Assets	£	£	£
Fixed assets	Cost	Depreciation	Net value
Machinery	50000	8000	42000
Fixtures and fittings	20000	2000	18000
Vehicles	25000	6000	19000
	95000	16000	79000
Current assets			
Stock		20000	
Debtors	6000		
less: Provision for Doubtful			
Debts	300		
	5700		
less: Provision for Discounts	114	5586	
Insurance prepaid		84	
Bank		8000	
Cash		500	34170
			113170

In any balance sheet which has been correctly drawn up, total assets
will always equal the sum of capital and liabilities. This is the rule
enunciated in the accounting concept known as the **dual aspect
concept**, but in any case it can be deduced from the double entry
principle. This provides a basis for a useful technique in **incomplete
records** accounting.

Many small traders maintain only a rudimentary record of their
business transactions. This presents a problem when a statement of

profit is required for taxation or other purposes, because it is often impossible to construct a Trading and Profit and Loss Account. However, if the trader has a reasonably accurate idea of the value of his assets and liabilities both at the beginning and at the end of the year, and if he also knows how much money he has drawn from the business during the year, it will be possible to arrive at an acceptable estimate of his profit.

Suppose that T. Anderson, a small trader in scrap metal, is able to provide the following valuations for his assets and liabilities at 1 January and 31 December:

January 1   *Assets:* Vehicle £3000, Equipment £2000, Stock
             £4500, Debtors £200, Bank £1000, Cash £90
             Liabilities: Creditors £1500, Rent Owing £100
December 31 *Assets:* Vehicle £2500, Equipment £4000, Stock
             £5000, Debtors £300, Bank £700, Cash £80,
             Insurance prepaid £120
             Liabilities: Creditors £1200

He is also able to demonstrate that he has taken £3000 for his use from the business during the year.

The first step is to construct what is known as a **Statement of Affairs**, in order to establish his capital balance at the beginning of the year. This takes the form of a rough balance sheet.

Statement of Affairs of T. Anderson as at 1 January 1985

	£	£
Assets		
Fixed Assets		
Vehicle	3000	
Equipment	2000	5000
Current Assets		
Stock	4500	
Debtors	200	
Bank	1000	
Cash	90	5790
		10790
Capital and liabilities		
Capital		9190[1]
Liabilities		
Trade creditors	1500	
Expense creditors (Rent)	100	1600
		10790

Workings

(1) The capital figure (£9190) is arrived at by deducting the value of the liabilities (£1600) from assets total (£10790).

The next step is to construct a formal balance sheet for the end of the year, incorporating this opening capital balance.

Balance Sheet of T. Anderson
as at 31 December 1985

	£	£
Capital and liabilities		
Capital		9190
add: Profit		5310
		14500
less: Drawings		3000
		11500
Liabilities		
Creditors		1200
		12700
Assets		
Fixed assets		
Vehicles	2500	
Equipment	4000	6500
Current assets		
Stock	5000	
Debtors	300	
Insurance prepaid	120	
Bank	700	
Cash	80	6200
		12700

The profit is calculated by working backwards to find the missing figure:

	£
Total capital plus liabilities	12700
(because capital plus liabilities = assets)	
less: Creditors	1200
	11500
add: Drawings	3000
	14500
less: Opening capital	9190
Profit	5310

The balance sheet of a partnership

A partnership, as the name implies, is a firm whose ownership is shared by two or more persons. Each of the partners will have made his own contribution towards the investment in the firm, and this means that separate Capital Accounts will have to be maintained. Furthermore, the firm's accounts will have to reflect the arrangements which the partners have come to among themselves about the sharing of the net profit. The ratio in which profit is shared among – or 'appropriated to' – individual partners is not usually decided only on the basis of the size of their individual cash contributions – technical expertise and other skills can be equally important considerations – so the process of allocating the profit must allow for a number of different requirements.

Because the profit share itself is not directly related to the size of capital investment, most partnership agreements include a clause providing that partners will receive interest at a certain fixed rate on their capital balances. It is also normal procedure to charge partners interest on money they withdraw from the firm during the course of the year. Often, too, a salary will be paid to one or more of the partners. The **Appropriation Account** is used to give effect to these provisions.

Suppose that the trial balance at the beginning of this chapter had been extracted from the books of the partnership of Black, White and Grey, but that the capital element was not £80000 but £90000, made up of the following capital balances:

Capital: Black	£40000
Capital: White	£30000
Capital: Grey	£20000

Suppose also that the partners had agreed: (i) to share profits in the ratio of 2:1:1 (that is 2/4, 1/4 and 1/4, or 1/2, 1/4 and 1/4); (ii) to pay Grey a salary of £3000 a year; (iii) to pay interest on capital at the rate of 5% on balances at the beginning of the year; and (iv) to charge interest on drawings at 2½%. We will assume that net profit for the year was £15000 and that drawings by the partners amounted to: Black £5000, White £4000 and Grey £3000.

Appropriation Account

	£	£	£
Net profit (from Profit and Loss Account)			15000
less: Interest on capital: Black	2000		
White	1500		
Grey	1000	4500	
Salary: Grey		3000	7500
add: Interest on drawings: Black		125	
White		100	
Grey		75	300
			7800
less: Profit: Black		3900	
White		1950	
Grey		1950	7800

The Capital Accounts will now appear as:

Capital: Black

	£		£
Drawings	5000	Balance b/d	40000
Appropriation:		Appropriation:	
Interest on		Interest	2000
drawings	125	Profit	3900
Balance c/d	40775		
	45900		45900
		Balance b/d	40775

Capital: White

	£		£
Drawings	4000	Balance b/d	30000
Appropriation:		Appropriation:	
Interest on		Interest	1500
drawings	100	Profit	1950
Balance c/d	29350		
	33450		33450
		Balance b/d	29350

Capital: Grey

	£		£
Drawings	3000	Balance b/d	20000
Appropriation:		Appropriation:	
Interest on		Interest	1000
drawings	75	Salary	3000
Balance c/d	22875	Profit	1950
	25950		25950
		Balance b/d	22875

(In practice, many partnerships prefer to maintain their Capital Accounts intact and to use what are known as **Current Accounts** to record entries from the Appropriation Account and the Drawings Account. This is a technicality which involves no new principles and need not detain us.)

**Balance Sheet of Black, White and Grey
as at 31 December 1985**

	£	£	£
Capital: Black	40775		
White	29350		
Grey	22875		93000
Long-term liability			
Loan – Green			20000
Current liabilities			
Trade creditors		10000	
Expense creditors (Rent)		170	10170
			123170

In almost every respect the assets section of the balance sheet of a partnership will be identical with that of a sole trader. The single exception is the treatment of *goodwill*. Goodwill can be briefly described as that part of the total value of a firm which is not represented by the value of its physical assets. Obviously every firm which can expect to continue in business making a satisfactory profit has a value which is greater than the sum of its fixed and current assets. This extra 'non-physical' value is difficult to quantify because of the number, and the constantly changing character, of the factors which affect it – the possession of special trading advantages, a favourable site, unusual managerial expertise, to name only a few. Ultimately, the goodwill of a firm at any point in time depends on the price which would be realized if the firm were sold at that moment. In the example we are considering, if Black, White and Grey knew that they could sell their firm for £10000 more than the value of its physical assets, then this would be the value of its goodwill.

Goodwill is important to a partnership because every partner has a claim on it in proportion to his share of profit. Thus, if Black, who receives a one-half share of the firm's profits, decided to retire, he would expect to be paid out, in addition to the balance on his Capital

Account, half of the value of the goodwill of the partnership on the date of his retirement. Similarly, if a new partner, Brown, joined the firm, he would be expected to *pay in* a proportion of the goodwill equal to his profit share, in addition to his capital investment, on the principle that he would be acquiring a claim on the profit which would be realized on the sale of business. Goodwill must therefore be valued as accurately as possible whenever the legal relationships between partners change in any way. This sometimes involves opening a special Goodwill Account in the books. Where this is the case, goodwill will be shown as the first of the fixed assets in the balance sheet.

Assets	Cost	Depreciation	Net value
Fixed assets			
Goodwill	10000	–	10000
Machinery	50000	8000	42000
Fixtures and fittings	20000	2000	18000
Vehicles	25000	6000	19000
	105000	16000	89000
Current assets			
Stock		20000	
Debtors	6000		
less: Provision for Doubtful Debts	300		
	5700		
less: Provision for Discount	114	5586	
Insurance prepaid		84	
Bank		8000	
Cash		500	34170
			123170

Total assets again equal the sum of capital and liabilities. It may be wondered how this can be the case if a sum of £10000 has been introduced into the assets as goodwill. The reason is that the Goodwill Account debit balance will have been created by journal transaction crediting each of the partners' Capital Accounts with a share of goodwill determined by their profit-sharing ratio. Thus, Black's Capital Account balance is £5000 more than would otherwise have been the case; and White and Grey also have each benefited to the extent of £2500.

The balance sheet of a limited liability company

The ownership and control of a company is shared by a far greater number of investors than is the case with a partnership, and it would be a matter of great difficulty to maintain separate Capital Accounts for each owner. In fact these separate accounts are not necessary because, unlike partners who are 'jointly and severally' liable for the debts of the partnership, the liability of contributors to the capital of a company is limited to the amount of money they invest in the company. No further record of their individual liability is needed beyond what is already provided in the company's Share Register.

Every company is required to declare the full amount of capital it proposes to raise – and therefore the maximum liability it intends to incur – in the **Memorandum of Association** which is drawn up as part of the process of incorporation. This is known as the company's **authorized capital** and it will appear under this title at the top of the capital and liabilities section of the balance sheet. The company is also required to declare the composition of its authorized capital, i.e. to indicate the type or types, and the unit values, of the shares it proposes to issue. Shares can be of different types but only two classes are in common use and therefore need to be considered. **Preference shares** are shares whose owners are entitled to a share of profits at a fixed rate of return; thus the owner of 10 000 12% preference shares with a nominal value of £1 each will be paid £1 200. **Ordinary shares** do not attract a fixed rate of return; their owners are paid a **dividend**, or share of the taxed profits, at a rate which is fixed each year by the directors of the company, after the preference shareholders have been paid.

It is the **issued capital** of the firm which constitutes the company's capital investment, and this need not equal the authorized capital. A company which has an authorized capital of, say, 50 000 preference shares and 100 000 ordinary shares, both of £1 each, may have issued 30 000 preference shares and 70 000 ordinary shares. This would appear in the balance sheet as follows:

Capital and liabilities

Authorized capital

	£
50 000 12% Preference Shares of £1 each	50 000
100 000 Ordinary Shares of £1 each	100 000
	150 000

Issued capital

30 000 12% Preference Shares of £1 each	30 000
70 000 Ordinary Shares of £1 each	70 000
	100 000

The authorized capital figure is not included in the addition of capital and liabilities; it is shown only as an item of information and is not part of the capital raised by the company.

When a company has been in existence for a number of years and has established a successful trading record, its shares will tend to increase in value; investors, that is, will be prepared to pay, say, £1.50 for a share which was originally issued at £1. If this were so in the case of the company we are considering and this company wished to raise further capital by increasing its issued ordinary capital up to the maximum permitted by its authorized ordinary capital, then it would obviously price its new issue of 30 000 ordinary shares at £1.50. (If it did not do this, investors would simply buy the shares at £1 and immediately resell them at a profit of 50%.) The funds received from the issue would therefore amount to £45 000, a gain of £15 000 on the nominal issue. The law requires that only the nominal value of the issue be shown as issued capital in the balance sheet; any money paid by shareholders above this amount must be credited to a **Share Premium Account**. The Share Premium Account is an example of what is known as a **capital reserve** – that is money put aside, usually to comply with some requirement of the Companies Act, which may not be used for purposes of distribution of profit.

Not all reserves are subject to this restriction. The company may, in a good year, wish to put aside a certain amount of the current year's profit to a **General** or **Revenue Reserve**, specifically in order to ensure that funds will be available for distribution as dividends in future years when trading results may not be as good. As in the case of partnership accounting, this and other allocations of profit are effected by means of an Appropriation Account.

Let us assume that the company in our example has made a trading profit of £80000 for the year, half of which must be set aside as a provision for taxation. Of the remainder, £20000 is to be used to create a General Reserve, preference shareholders are to be paid the dividend due to them, and 15 pence in the pound (on the *nominal* value) is to be paid to ordinary shareholders. The balance on the Appropriation Account is to be carried forward to the following year.

Appropriation Account

	£	£
Net profit (from Profit and Loss Account)		80000
less: Provision for taxation		40000
		40000
less: Transfer to General Reserve	20000	
Preference dividend due (12% of £30000)	3600	
Proposed ordinary dividend (15% of £70000)	10500	34100
Balance carried forward		5900

Each of these items will have an effect on the balance sheet; but before this can be demonstrated it will be necessary to consider the treatment of long-term liabilities. Loans raised by companies usually take the form of **debentures**, that is loan certificates issued in much the same way as preference shares, usually for unit values of £1, £5 or £10 and at a predetermined rate of interest. They differ from preference shares in two important ways: (i) they are not part of capital; and (ii) the interest due to them must be paid, whether or not a profit has been recorded for the current year. Interest on debentures is therefore a charge against the Profit and Loss Account and does not appear in the Appropriation Account. Let us say that in this case the company had issued 50000 10% debentures of £1 each and that current liabilities, apart from Appropriation Account items, were trade creditors £20000 and expense creditors £300:

**Balance Sheet of ABC Ltd
as at 31 December 1985**

	£	£
Capital and liabilities		
Authorized capital		
50000 12% Preference shares of £1 each		50000
100000 Ordinary shares of £1 each		100000

Issued capital		
30 000 12% Preference shares of £1 each		30 000
70 000 Ordinary shares of £1 each		70 000
		100 000
Reserves		
Share Premium Account		15 000
General Reserve		20 000
Retained earnings (balance on Appropriation Account)		5 900
Shareholders' funds		140 900
Debentures		
50 000 10% Debentures of £1 each		50 000
Current liabilities		
Provision for taxation	40 000	
Preference dividend due	3 600	
Proposed ordinary dividend	10 000	
Trade creditors	20 000	
Expense creditors	300	73 900
		264 800

The assets side of a company balance sheet is essentially the same
as that of a partnership, as will be seen from Example 6.1. It should
be pointed out, however, that the balance sheet is presented here in
the form in which it would be compiled for a company's own inter-
nal use. No attempt has been made to conform to the intricate
requirements of the Companies' Act governing the *publication* of
company final accounts.

Example 6.1. The Progressive Company Limited has an authorized
share capital of 500 000 12% Preference shares of £1 each, and
1 000 000 Ordinary shares of £1 each. The balances on the books for
the year ended 31 December 1985, after completion of the Trading
and Profit and Loss Account, were as follows:

	Dr	Cr
	£	£
Preference share capital		400 000
Ordinary share capital		900 000
Profit and Loss Appropriation Account		10 000
General Reserve		30 000
Net profit for the year ended 31 December 1985		320 000
Premises (at cost)	1 200 000	
Delivery vans (at cost)	120 000	
Fixtures and fittings (at cost)	75 000	
Provisions for depreciation:		
Vans		35 000
Fixtures and Fittings		20 000

Cash at bank	340000	
Cash in hand	14000	
Trade debtors	28000	
Provision for Doubtful Debts		2000
Creditors		10000
Accrued expenses		2000
Stocks	51000	
Payment in advance	1000	
15% Debentures		100000
	1829000	1829000

The directors propose to pay the preference dividend, a dividend of 20 pence in the pound, to the ordinary shareholders, and to transfer £50000 to the General Reserve.

Prepare the Profit and Loss Appropriation Account and the balance sheet for the company.

Solution

Appropriation Account

	£	£
Balance brought forward from 1984		10000
add: Net profit 1985		320000
		330000
less: Preference dividend	48000	
Proposed ordinary dividend	180000	
Transfer to General Reserve	50000	278000
Balance carried forward		52000

Balance sheet of the Progressive Trading Company Limited as at 31 December 1985

	£	£	£
Capital and liabilities			
Authorized capital			
500000 12% Preference shares of £1 each			500000
1000000 Ordinary shares of £1 each			1000000
			1500000
Issued capital			
400000 12% Preference shares of £1 each			400000
900000 Ordinary shares of £1 each			900000
			1300000
Reserves			
General reserve			80000
Retained earnings			52000
Shareholders' funds			1432000
15% Debentures			100000

Current liabilities		
Preference dividend due	48000	
Proposed ordinary dividend	180000	
Trade creditors	10000	
Expense creditors	2000	240000
		1772000

Assets

Fixed assets	Cost	Depreciation	Net value
Premises	1200000	–	1200000
Delivery vans	120000	35000	85000
Fixtures and fittings	75000	20000	55000
	1395000	55000	1340000

Current assets		
Stock		51000
Debtors	28000	
less: Provision for doubtful debts	2000	26000
Prepaid expenses		1000
Bank		340000
Cash		14000
		432000
		1772000

Exercises

Exercise 6.1. The partnership of Jerome, George and Harris, trading as Thames Excursions, has the following balances remaining in the books after the completion of its Trading and Profit and Loss Account for the year ended 31 December 1984.

	Dr	Cr
	£	£
Capital: Jerome		30000
George		15000
Harris		10000
Equipment	29000	
Vehicles	15000	
Provisions for depreciation:		
Equipment		6000
Vehicles		4000
Debtors	8000	
Stock	19000	
Bank	3000	
Drawings: Jerome	4000	
George	2000	
Harris	1800	
Loan: Montmorency		5000
Provision for doubtful debts		150
Creditors		2000
Prepaid insurance	350	

Net profit for the year amounted to £10000. The partners
have agreed to share profits in the ratio 3:1:1, to allow
interest of 5% on capital balances at the beginning of the
year, to charge 2½% interest on drawings and to pay Harris
an annual salary of £2000.

Prepare the Appropriation Account, partners' Capital
Accounts and Balance Sheet.

Exercise 6.2.   From the following balances in the books of Dombey
and Son Limited prepare the Appropriation Account and
Balance Sheet as at 30 June 1985:

	Dr	Cr
	£	£
Premises (at cost)	230000	
Provision for doubtful debts		1500
Provision for depreciation on vehicles		3500
Vehicles	70000	
Profit and Loss Account (Net profit)		80000
Provision for Discounts Allowed		1200
Bank	5000	
Stock	15000	
Debtors and creditors	36200	22000
General Reserve		23000
12% Debentures		75000
20000 10% Preference shares		20000
100000 Ordinary shares		100000
Share Premium Account		30000
	356200	356200

Notes
(1) The Company's authorized capital was:
     40000 10% preference shares of £1 each
     100000 ordinary shares of £1 each.
(2) The preference dividend and an ordinary dividend of 15 pence in
     the pound are to be paid.
(3) £10000 is to be transferred to General Reserve.

3 The Interpretative Function

7 Understanding Business Reports: Ratio Analysis

The need for interpretation

A firm's final accounts do more than indicate its present financial condition and its profit for the year. Accounting has developed techniques of interpretation which enable an experienced analyst to extract much more information from a balance sheet than is immediately evident, particularly if the previous year's revenue accounts are also available. This information is especially valuable to management itself as a guide to the firm's progress and its relative stability from year to year. It is also useful to other persons and institutions with an interest in the firm, particularly shareholders, potential investors, bank managers and creditors.

Profitability criteria

It is normally expected of any business in the private sector that it should be profitable, at least in the long run. If it is not, its resources are being misused and could be put to better use elsewhere. Now simply to say that a trader has made a profit of £15 000 in any one year is not saying very much about the profitability of his firm. A number of other things have to be considered. What is the value of the owner's investment in the firm? What kind of return could he have got from putting his capital into some other form of investment? How does his firm's performance compare with that of other firms of the same size in the same industrial or commercial sector? Is his profit this year better than it was last year?

The technique known as **ratio analysis** answers these questions by assessing the relationships between individual items in the balance sheet, and the final accounts of the firm generally, and considering the significance of these relationships. It is a technique which can be used to analyse firms of any type or structure; however, because it is employed to greatest effect in the study of limited liability companies, we shall be discussing it in that context in this chapter.

Example 7.1. Consider the following summarized balance sheets of H. Thompson Ltd for Year 1 and Year 2, which have been arranged in adjacent columns to facilitate comparison. An adaptation has also been made in regard to current liabilities, which in this example are shown as a deduction from current assets instead of being included in the capital and liabilities section. This is one of a number of possible variations in the presentation of a balance sheet, and it has the advantage of emphasizing the importance of **working capital** (current assets minus current liabilities), a concept we shall be examining later in the chapter.

		Year 1		Year 2
	£	£	£	£
Issued capital		100000		150000
Reserves				
Share premium		–		10000
General reserve		20000		30000
Profit and loss		5000		15000
		125000		205000
12% Debentures		–		45000
		125000		250000
Assets				
Fixed assets				
Vehicles (less depreciation)		30000		90000
Fixtures (less depreciation)		10000		25000
		40000		115000
Current assets				
Stock	40000		90000	
Debtors	50000		110000	
Bank	15000		5000	
	105000		205000	
less: Current liabilities				
Trade creditors	20000		70000	
		85000		135000
		125000		250000

The following additional information is available:

	Year 1 £	Year 2 £
Sales: Cash	100000	150000
Credit	300000	550000
Cost of goods sold	240000	413000
Expenses (excluding interest)	130000	241600
Debenture interest	—	5400
Ordinary dividends	15000	20000
Opening stock	30000	40000
Opening debtors	40000	50000
Market price of ordinary shares	£1.20	£1.50
Issued capital:		
10% Preference shares of £1 each	£20000	£20000
Ordinary shares of £1 each	£80000	£130000

(A) The primary ratio

The primary test of profitability is the **return on capital employed** or **ROCE**. This ratio can have different meanings, depending on the purpose of the analysis. We shall assume for the moment that the objective is to discover the relationship between the firm's earnings in the way of profit, and the resources available to it as fixed assets and working capital. This can be expressed by the formula:

$$\frac{\text{Net profit}}{\text{Fixed assets} + \text{Working capital}} \times 100$$

Net profit can be calculated by subtracting the cost of goods sold and expenses from total sales, in the listing above, and the sum of fixed assets and working capital is derived directly from the balance sheet.

Applied to our data, the formula gives the following results:

	Year 1 £	Year 2 £
Return on capital employed	$\frac{30000}{125000} \times 100 = 24\%$	$\frac{45400}{250000} \times 100 = 18.16\%$

The downward trend in the ROCE indicates a decline in profitability. The firm's investment in its fixed assets and working capital – represented on the balance sheet by its issued capital, reserves and debentures – earned a return of 24% in Year 1, but only 18.16% in Year 2. (Note: The calculation of the return for Year 2 is complicated by the need to take account of the fact that the capital employed in that year includes £45 000 debentures. This means that the debenture interest of £5 400, which is a charge against profit and loss, has had to be added back to the net profit (i) because it is itself part of the return on capital employed – as the return accruing to the debenture holders – and (ii) because to deduct it from profit would distort the comparison of trading results. This complication has been introduced into the example as a warning of the complexity of ratio analysis and of the dangers which can arise from indiscriminately applying simple formulae.)

(B) The secondary ratios

Having measured the trend in profitability, we must now attempt to discover its cause. The return on capital employed expresses the relationship between net profit and **net assets** (the term we shall use from now on to denote fixed assets plus working capital), which means that the change in the ROCE can be traced to changes in these two variables. If we relate each of them to the firm's sales figure for the year, we obtain two very useful **secondary ratios** which, taken together, explain the change in the ROCE:

(1) The **net profit percentage** (NP%) is simply net profit (NP) expressed as a percentage of sales. For the two years this results in:

$$\text{Year 1} \qquad\qquad\qquad \text{Year 2}$$

$$\text{NP\%} = \frac{30\,000}{400\,000} \times 100 = 7.5\% \quad \frac{45\,400}{700\,000} \times 100 = 6.5\%$$

The profit margin has fallen by 1.0 percentage point.

(2) The ratio known as **asset turnover** measures the relationship between the company's investment in its net assets and the sales revenue produced by this investment. This is expressed by the formula:

$$\text{Asset turnover (AT)} = \frac{\text{Sales (S)}}{\text{Net assets (NA)}}$$

When applied to the two years, this gives:

	Year 1	Year 2
	£	£

$$\text{AT} = \frac{400\,000}{125\,000} = 3.2 \qquad \frac{700\,000}{250\,000} = 2.8$$

There has been a decline in the efficiency of the firm's use of its assets. Whereas in Year 1 each £1 worth of investment in assets was producing £3.2 worth of sales, only £2.8 worth of sales was being produced in Year 2.

The relationship between the return on capital employed and the secondary ratios can be demonstrated mathematically:

$$\text{(ROCE)} \frac{\text{NP} \times 100}{\text{NA}} = \text{(NP\%)} \frac{\text{NP} \times 100}{\text{S}} \times \text{(AT)} \frac{\text{S}}{\text{NA}}$$

Inserting the values for Year 1, we have:

$$\text{ROCE} = 7.5\% \times 3.2 = 24\%$$

which is the figure we arrived at earlier.

Overall, it can be said that the decline in the company's return on its capital has been caused by both a fall of 1.0 percentage point in net profit and a 12½% decrease in the efficiency of its use of assets.

(C) The tertiary ratios

We have now come some way in our analysis of the profitability of H. Thompson Ltd, but we have by no means completed the process. The changes in the secondary ratios have yet to be examined.

(1) Expense ratios

Since net profit is what remains when expenses have been deducted from sales, it follows that any variation in the ratio of individual

expenses to sales will affect the net profit percentage. The best way
to examine these changes is to convert each of the firm's expenses
to a percentage of sales and then to study significant variations in
these percentages between the years. Of course this will be possible
only if the analyst has access to the firm's Trading and Profit and
Loss Accounts. Let us suppose that this is the case and that the
following table has been prepared:

	Year 1		Year 2		Change
	£	%	£	%	% points
Sales	400000	100.0	700000	100.0	–
Cost of goods sold	240000	60.0	413000	59.0	−1.0
Gross profit	160000	40.0	287000	41.0	+1.0
Expenses:					
Wages	72000	18.0	128700	18.4	+0.4
Rent	20000	5.0	35000	5.0	–
Electricity	19200	4.8	43000	6.1	+1.3
Depreciation	8000	2.0	23000	3.3	+1.3
General expenses	10800	2.7	11900	1.7	−1.0
Net profit (plus interest)	30000	7.5	45400	6.5	−1.0

Downward changes in the cost of sales and general expenses have
been more than offset by increases in wages, rent and depreciation.
This explains the fall in net profit percentage from 7.5% to 6.5%.

(2) *Asset turnover ratios*

Inefficiency in the use of assets can be traced to individual assets by
relating each of them either to sales or to the cost of sales, and then
comparing the ratios for the two years.

(i) **Sales to fixed asset ratios**   Judgements based on comparisons of
fixed assets with sales can be somewhat arbitrary. An investment in
staff amenities, for example, may be very much in the long-term
interests of the firm, but it is unlikely that the benefit will be directly
reflected by an increase in the sales figure for the year in which the
investment is made. Nevertheless, fixed assets are costly investments and it is important to keep the efficiency of their utilization
under constant review. In our example, the ratios are:

	Year 1	Year 2	Change
	£	£	%

Vehicles $\dfrac{400\,000}{30\,000} = 13.3$ $\dfrac{700\,000}{90\,000} = 7.7$ -5.6

Fixtures $\dfrac{400\,000}{10\,000} = 40.0$ $\dfrac{700\,000}{25\,000} = 28.0$ -12.0

At first sight, there appears to have been a marked decrease in the efficiency of use of these two assets. However, before concluding that either the investment should not have been made or that the targeted sales figure for Year 2 has not been achieved, two important points must be borne in mind. First, the information gives no indication of the dates on which the investments were made in these assets. If, for example, they were both bought in November, they could have had little effect on sales, and the comparison becomes meaningless. Secondly, investments in fixed assets are usually planned in accordance with long-term budgets, and their full impact on the volume of sales would not normally be expected to become apparent in the year of their purchase.

(ii) **Sales to current asset ratios**

   (a) **Stock turnover** This important ratio relates the stocks maintained by the firm to its sales for the year. The first difficulty in attempting to calculate this ratio is encountered when deciding on the value to attribute to the asset. The year-end closing stock figure is not satisfactory because it will probably not reflect a typical value as a result of year-end sales and other measures taken in preparation for a new year's trading. The ideal would be an average month-end figure, but the information required for this calculation is usually not available. The conventional method is to add the opening stock for the year to the closing stock and divide this result by two. This 'average stock' is then compared with the cost of sales for the year to establish the **rate of stock turnover**. In the case of H. Thompson Ltd this would be:

$$\frac{\text{Cost of goods sold}}{\text{Average stock}}$$

	Year 1		Year 2	Change
	£		£	

$$\frac{240000}{(30000 + 40000) \div 2} = 6.9 \qquad \frac{413000}{(40000 + 90000) \div 2} = 6.4 \qquad -0.5$$

This rate of stock turnover can be said to mean that the firm sold its stocks and replaced them 6.9 times in Year 1 and 6.4 times during Year 2. The change of −0.5 is an unfavourable trend, indicating a deterioration in the sales activity of the firm.

The ratio can then be used to calculate the **stock turnover period**, that is, the time taken by the firm to dispose of average stock. This is done by dividing the turnover ratio into the months, weeks or days of the year, thus:

	Year 1	Year 2
Stock turnover ratio:	6.9	6.4

Stock turnover period: $\dfrac{52}{6.9} = 7.5$ weeks $\qquad \dfrac{52}{6.4} = 8.1$ weeks

Obviously, the shorter the time taken to sell off stocks the better, so the result for Year 2 is a deterioration on the result for Year 1.

(b) **Debtor turnover**   The information available to us on H. Thompson Ltd tells us that, of the total sales increase of £300000 in Year 2, £250000 was accounted for by credit sales, and that the debtor asset in the balance sheet increased by £60000 during the year. There is an obvious relationship between these two variables and it needs careful attention. In enlarging its credit sales, the company has increased its investment in what amounts to loans to customers, to enable them to purchase its goods. It is therefore using funds which could have been employed in the *production* of goods for sale for the direct *promotion* of sales. The success or otherwise of this policy can be measured by the **debtor turnover ratio**, which relates the value of credit sales to the firm's average debtors. The same problem of defining averages arises here as was encountered in attempting to evaluate average stock, and the same rule is applied: add the opening and closing values and divide by two. In our example this becomes:

$$\text{Debtor turnover} = \frac{\text{Credit sales}}{\text{Average debtors}}$$

	Year 1		Year 2
	£		£

$$\frac{300000}{(40000 + 50000) \div 2} = 6.70 \qquad \frac{550000}{(50000 + 110000) \div 2} = 6.88$$

On the basis of these calculations, it could be said that, whereas in Year 1 every £1 worth of investment in debtors was producing £6.70 worth of credit sales, the same investment was producing £6.88 in Year 2.

The ratio can also be used to measure the effectiveness of the firm's credit management, by determining the **debtor turnover period**. This is calculated, as in the case of the stock turnover period, by dividing the number of months, weeks or days in the year by the ratio:

	Year 1	Year 2
Debtor turnover ratio:	6.70	6.88

Debtor turnover period: $\dfrac{52}{6.70} = 7.8$ weeks $\quad \dfrac{52}{6.88} = 7.6$ weeks

This is taken to indicate that, whereas in Year 1 debtors were, on average, settling their accounts every 7.8 weeks, in Year 2 they were doing so in 7.6 weeks, a marginal improvement.

Solvency criteria

In addition to being profitable, a firm must also be *solvent*; that is to say, it must be able to meet its obligations to its creditors. It does not follow as a matter of course that a profitable company will automatically remain solvent. A company which expands its operations without taking care to ensure that its cash resources are sufficient to meet its day-to-day expenditure requirements will not last very long, no matter how glittering its profit potential may be.

The resources which the firm has at its disposal to meet its daily needs are together known as its **working capital**, which is defined as current assets minus current liabilities. Current assets, as we know from our discussion on the balance sheet, are made up of stock, debtors, bank and cash. Of these, bank and cash represent money which is immediately available; debtors will usually settle their accounts within the coming month; and a regular flow of cash is being generated by the turnover of stock. The first call on the money derived from these sources is, of course, the firm's current liabilities: its creditors and accrued expenses, short-term obligations which must usually be settled within the coming month.

(A) Working capital ratio, or current ratio

The first test of a firm's solvency is its **working capital ratio**, sometimes also known as its **current ratio**. This is expressed by the formula:

$$\text{Working capital ratio} = \frac{\text{Current assets}}{\text{Current liabilities}}$$

In our example the figures would be:

Year 1	Year 2
£	£
$\dfrac{105\,000}{20\,000} = 5.25$	$\dfrac{205\,000}{70\,000} = 2.93$

In both years, the result is well above the critical ratio of 1, so the firm is obviously in no danger of being unable to satisfy its creditors. It should be noticed, however, that a high working capital ratio, such as that shown here for Year 1, is not always a good thing inasmuch as it often indicates a wasteful use of resources. The £15 000 held in the current account at the bank seems to have been more than was actually required for immediate cash purposes, and the firm would probably have benefited from transferring much of it to a deposit account or some other investment from which interest could have been earned. It also seems likely that stocks were maintained at too high a level in Year 1, thus locking up funds which could also have been used more profitably elsewhere.

(B) *Liquid or acid-test ratio*

A more precise test of a firm's ability to pay its immediate obligations is provided by a ratio which does not include stock. The **liquid ratio** or **acid-test ratio** is defined as:

$$\frac{\text{Current assets} - \text{Stock}}{\text{Current Liabilities}}$$

Applied to our example this results in:

	Year 1		Year 2
	£		£

$$\frac{105\,000 - 40\,000}{20\,000} = 3.25 \qquad \frac{205\,000 - 90\,000}{70\,000} = 1.64$$

By this test, also, the firm is shown to be thoroughly solvent in both years.

Investment criteria

Shareholders and potential investors have an interest in the interpretation of a company's balance sheet which is not entirely satisfied by the criteria we have been discussing. They will wish to be assured not merely that the company is profitable and solvent in itself but also that the return it offers to its investors is both adequate and safe. Further tests therefore have to be applied.

Earnings per share

Ownership of a limited liability company is vested ultimately in its ordinary shareholders, and it is to them that the firm's profit belongs after all liabilities – including taxation – have been met and any dividends due to preference shareholders have been paid. The **earnings per share ratio** is calculated by dividing this residual profit by the *number* (not the value) of ordinary shares issued by the company:

$$\frac{\text{Net profit} - \text{Taxation} - \text{Preference dividend}}{\text{Number of ordinary shares}}$$

Assuming the taxation paid to have been £10000 in Year 1 and £15000 in Year 2, this would result in the following ratios for H. Thompson Ltd:

Year 1   Year 2

£   £

$$\frac{30000 - 10000 - 2000}{80000} = 22.5p \qquad \frac{40000 - 15000 - 2000}{130000} = 17.7p$$

Between Year 1 and Year 2, the return accruing to each ordinary share with a nominal value of £1 decreased from 22.5 pence to 17.7 pence.

Dividend yield

The market price of a share will only rarely be equal to its nominal value. A company's shares will be in greater demand as it becomes more profitable, and this increase in demand will determine the share price. The earnings-per-share ratio is not therefore an accurate indication of the income derived from the amount actually invested. This is usually measured by what is known as the **dividend yield ratio**:

$$\frac{\text{Dividend per share}}{\text{Market price per share}}$$

Investors who know how much they have paid for their shares will be able to calculate this ratio precisely. For the company as a whole, an approximate indicator can be obtained by dividing the dividend per share by the market price per share. In the case of H. Thompson Ltd, the ordinary dividend per share was 18.75 pence (£15000 divided by 80000 shares) in Year 1, and 15.38 pence (£20000 divided by 130000 shares) in Year 2. The dividend yield would therefore be:

Year 1   Year 2

$$\frac{18.75 \text{ pence}}{120 \text{ pence}} \times 100 = 15.62\% \qquad \frac{15.38 \text{ pence}}{150 \text{ pence}} \times 100 = 10.25\%$$

These results indicate that the return on the investment as represented by the actual income received by shareholders has declined. This has been caused partly by the rise in the market price of the share and partly by the directors' decision to distribute a lower percentage of profit as dividend. This retention of profit is reflected in the higher balances shown against the General Reserve and the Profit and Loss Account on the balance sheet. It is the way in which profit is re-invested in the business. It benefits the shareholders because it provides the capital for the production of profits and therefore enhances the value of their shares.

Price earnings ratio

The **price earnings ratio (PER)** is a convenient way of relating the profit record of a company, as represented by its earnings per share after taxation, to the market price of its shares.

$$\frac{\text{Market price per share}}{\text{Earnings per share}}$$

In the case of H. Thompson Ltd, the PER for each year was:

$$\text{Year 1} \qquad\qquad \text{Year 2}$$

$$\frac{£1.20}{22.5 \text{ pence}} = 5.3 \qquad \frac{£1.50}{17.6 \text{ pence}} = 8.5$$

The significance of this ratio is best explained by saying that the cost of a share purchased in Year 1 would, at the rate of earnings prevailing in that year, have been recovered in 5.3 years, whereas the period of recovery of the cost of a share bought in Year 2 would have been 8.5 years.

The limitations of ratio analysis

Ratio analysis is an indispensable technique in the interpretation of business reports, but it is subject to serious limitations which must be borne in mind if misleading conclusions are to be avoided. The most obvious limitation is that no accounting statement can ever provide a complete picture of any business; many important aspects of a firm which have a crucial bearing on its profit potential cannot be deduced from a balance sheet. The **concept of money measurement** makes this explicit when it states that accountants are concerned only with facts which can be expressed in monetary terms with an acceptable degree of precision. This automatically excludes any assessment of staff morale, expertise and other important business factors. Also, a firm's policies in regard to such matters as depreciation and stock valuation significantly affect its reported profit and asset values; unless these policies are known and allowed for, it will be impossible to make accurate comparisons between firms. Inter-firm comparisons are further complicated by the fact that there may be considerable differences between organizations both in size and in the nature of their trading activities, even when they operate within the same business category; and these differences may not be evident in their published reports. For these and other reasons — some of which will be apparent from what has already been explained in this chapter — interpretations which are derived purely from the calculations of ratios should be treated as only partial explanations and should be supplemented, wherever possible, with information derived from other sources.

Exercise

Exercise 7.1. Mr Jones, a retired businessman with £10000 to invest, is considering buying shares in one of two retail companies, ABC Ltd and XYZ Ltd. On the basis of the following information, how would you advise him?

	ABC Ltd £	XYZ Ltd £
Sales: Cash	300000	100000
Credit	1000000	1500000
Cost of goods sold	900000	1000000
Expenses: Selling	180000	240000
Administration	110000	180000
Stock at 1 January	100000	220000
Debtors at 1 January	120000	140000
Ordinary dividend paid	60000	150000

Balance sheet at 31 December

	ABC Ltd		XYZ Ltd	
	£	£	£	£
Issued capital				
Ordinary shares		300000		500000
10% Preference shares		100000		–
		400000		500000
Reserves		100000		150000
		500000		650000
Assets				
Fixed assets				
Premises		200000		–
Fixtures and fittings		50000		220000
Vehicles		120000		260000
		370000		480000
Current Assets				
Stock	80000		280000	
Debtors	130000		160000	
Bank	40000		–	
	250000		440000	
less: Current liabilities				
Creditors	120000		230000	
Overdraft	–		40000	
Working capital		130000		170000
		500000		650000

8 Understanding Business Reports: Funds Flow Analysis

The need for interpretation

An inspection of the firm's final accounts, even with the use of ratio analysis, will not in itself tell the reader how the firm has used the financial resources available to it. If a profit has been earned, the cash flowing in as revenue will have exceeded the cash flowing out as expenses, and this will be evident in a general way. Except in very rare cases, however, the difference in the bank and cash balances between one year and the next will not equal the net cash inflow from profit. The fact that a business has made £25 000 profit this year, for example, will not necessarily mean that its bank balance will have gone up by £25 000. There are many **sources of funds** (receipts) and **applications of funds** (payments) which do not enter directly into the determination of profit, and these must be allowed for in considering how effectively (or otherwise) a firm has managed its funds.

Cash flow analysis

The kind of question people tend to ask about cash flow is: 'How is it that, although the firm has made a profit of £50 000 this year, its bank balance has fallen from £10 000 to an overdraft of £8 000?' The accounting technique of **cash flow analysis** explains the difference in cash and bank balances with a fair degree of precision. It does this, in principle, by comparing each asset and liability in the current year's balance sheet with the corresponding items in the previous year's balance sheet and then adding the sum of the differences between them to the current year's profit. This is set out as a **statement of sources and applications of funds** in which the difference between the sources and applications is shown to be equal to the change in the cash and bank balances.

Example 8.1. The following are the summarized balance sheets of a company for Year 1 and Year 2. We are asked to explain the change in the bank balance.

	£	Year 1 £	£	Year 2 £
Issued capital		250 000		350 000
Reserves				
Share premium		100 000		50 000
General reserve		40 000		50 000
Profit and loss		15 000		40 000
Shareholders' funds		405 000		490 000
15% Debentures		70 000		60 000
		475 000		550 000
Fixed assets				
Premises (at cost)		200 000		260 000
Machinery (at cost)	200 000		180 000	
less: Depreciation	40 000	160 000	50 000	130 000
		360 000		390 000
Current assets				
Stock	75 000		95 000	
Debtors	50 000		75 000	
Bank	20 000		50 000	
	145 000		220 000	
less: Current liabilities				
Trade creditors	30 000		60 000	
Working capital		115 000		160 000
		475 000		550 000

We are given the following additional information:

(a) Net profit from trading operations during Year 2 was £35 000

(b) Depreciation provided for the year was £17 000

(c) A machine which had originally cost £20 000 was sold during the year for £13 000. It had been depreciated by £7 000

The first step is to adjust the net profit figure by adding back the non-cash expenses – in this case, the depreciation for the year. This is because the transfer from the Profit and Loss Account to the Provision for Depreciation did not involve any actual payment – it was a journal transaction, not a Cash Book transaction – and we are trying to find the net *cash* inflow from the year's trading. The cash derived from other sources must then be added to the adjusted profit. These sources can be identified from: (i) *increases in capital or liabilities* – funds generated by new issues of shares or debentures, or by new credit facilities; and (ii) *decreases in assets* – the proceeds from the sale of fixed assets or the savings in bank expenditure arising from the reduction of investment in stocks or debtors.

The applications of funds, which are then deducted from the total sources, can be found in: (i) *decreases in capital or liabilities* – money expended on the reduction of preference share capital or debentures, or on reducing the firm's obligations to its creditors; and (ii) *increases in assets* – payments for the purchase of new fixed assets, or increased investment in stocks and debtors.

Statement of Sources and Applications of Funds:
Year ended 31 December, Year 2

	£	£
Sources of funds		
Net profit from trading	35000	
add: Depreciation	17000	52000
Funds from other sources:		
Issue of shares[1]	50000	
Sale of machine[2]	13000	
Increase in creditors	30000	93000
		145000
Applications of funds		
Redemption of debentures[3]	10000	
Purchase of premises	60000	
Increase in stock	20000	
Increase in debtors	25000	115000
Excess of sources over applications		30000
Increase in bank funds		
Bank balance 31 Dec Year 1	20000	
31 Dec Year 2	50000	30000

Notes

1. The issued capital has increased by £100000 which, at first sight, suggests that the company has received £100000 from a new issue of shares. However, the share premium balance has fallen by £50000, which can only mean that there has been a *capitalization of reserves* – a *bonus share issue*. Part of the funds represented by the Share Premium Account has been 'capitalized', that is transferred to issued capital by way of a free issue of shares to the company's existing shareholders in proportion to the number

of shares they already hold. Of the total increase in the company's share capital, therefore, only half represents money actually received.

2. The machine disposed of has been sold for a sum which is exactly equal to its cost, less the depreciation provided. If this had not been so, it would have been necessary to make some adjustment to the net profit for the year, to ensure that the profit or loss on disposal was not counted in twice, that is, included in both the net profit and the sale price of the asset.

3. The 15% debentures have decreased by £10 000. Debenture stock to this value must therefore have been *redeemed* – bought back by the company from its debenture holders.

It can be seen from this statement of sources and applications of funds that the company's trading activities for the year have resulted in a net cash inflow of £52 000 and that this has been augmented by funds received from the issue of new shares (£50 000) and the sale of a machine (£13 000). Furthermore the increase in the facilities available from creditors has meant that £30 000 which would have been expended on purchases has been retained in the bank. On the other hand, the company has purchased premises for £60 000, has spent £10 000 on the redemption of debentures and has increased its investments in stock (£20 000) and debtors (£25 000). The net effect of these movements of funds has been an increase of £30 000 in the company's bank balance.

Working capital flow analysis

The **working capital ratio** is the test normally applied in assessing a company's liquidity or solvency, and the analyst's attention is therefore likely to be concentrated more on the changes in working capital as a whole than on the increase or decrease in the firm's bank balance. This requires a different presentation in which the changes in only those items which are not part of working capital are included in the statement of sources and applications of funds. The difference between sources and applications is then shown as being equal to the net increase or decrease in working capital.

Example 8.2.

	£	£
Sources of funds		
Net profit from trading	35 000	
add: Depreciation	17 000	52 000
Funds from other sources:		
Issue of shares	50 000	
Sale of machine	13 000	63 000
		115 000
Applications of funds		
Redemption of debentures	10 000	
Purchase of premises	60 000	70 000
Excess of sources over applications		45 000
Increases/Decreases in working capital		
Increase in stock	20 000	
Increase in debtors	25 000	
Increase in bank	30 000	
	75 000	
less: Increase in creditors[1]	30 000	45 000

Note

1. Working capital is defined as current assets minus current liabilities. An increase in creditors (a current liability) is therefore a *decrease* in working capital

Working capital as a whole, as opposed to the bank balance, has increased by £45 000 over the year. This has happened because the *inflow* of funds from trading plus the proceeds from the issue of shares and the sale of a machine has exceeded the *outflow* of funds represented by the redemption of debentures and the purchase of new premises.

Exercise

Exercise 8.1.   Micawber Enterprises made a profit of £10 000 during the year ended 31 December 1986, but nevertheless both its bank balance and its working capital have decreased over the period. Using the following information, explain to Mr Micawber how this has come about.

	1985		1986	
	£	£	£	£
Assets employed				
Fixed assets, at cost		92000		106000
Depreciation		16000		18000
		76000		88000
Current assets				
Stocks	30000		35000	
Debtors	20000		17000	
Bank	5000		–	
	55000		52000	
Current liabilities				
Creditors	11000		15000	
Overdraft	–		12000	
Net current assets		44000		25000
		120000		113000
Financed by:				
Capital		91000		90000
add: Profit		8000		10000
		99000		100000
less: Drawings		9000		12000
		90000		88000
Loan		30000		25000
		120000		113000

Note

A machine which had cost £15000 and which had been depreciated by £5000 was sold for £12000.

4 The Predictive Function

9 Budgeting and Forecasting

The need for prediction

Up to this point our discussions have concentrated on the accounting treatment of historical transactions – transactions which have already taken place and the details of which are known with some certainty. We have seen how information on trading activity is recorded by double entries in the firm's ledgers, how this information is brought together in report form to disclose the firm's profit for the year, and finally how these reports can be interpreted to reveal how successful or otherwise the firm has been as a trading enterprise. But all of this would be of limited usefulness to business if accounting did not also provide some method of predicting, with a reasonable degree of accuracy, the firm's profitability and solvency within the *next* trading period. All investment in business is made with an eye to future income; the extent to which the future operations of a firm can be foreseen and planned is therefore a matter of profound importance.

Budgeting and forecasting

The planning of sales and production is determined in the first place by economic and technical considerations. There would be no point in producing 10000 units of a particular product unless the firm could be certain that there was a demand for that quantity

A.—8

of goods; nor could the firm contemplate production if such a target were beyond its technical competence or capacity. But if these requirements can be met, there remains the problem of ensuring that production is carried out in the most efficient and profitable way. This is the area of accounting called **management accounting,** a discipline which is concerned mainly with the application of **costing** techniques.

The first step in planning manufacturing activity is the co-ordination of the volume of production with the expected volume of sales. This involves close synchronization, if an even flow of production – with all that this entails for the efficient use of resources – is to be achieved. Suppose that the sales of a product for the six months of a budgeted period are expected to be:

	Jan	Feb	Mar	Apr	May	Jun
Sales (units)	800	700	950	1000	900	800

If the firm wishes to maintain a regular flow of production of, say, 850 units per month, while keeping a stock of at least 100 units in hand, then, as can be seen from the **production budget** below, the problem becomes one of calculating the stock of finished units with which the firm must *start* the budgeted period.

	Jan	Feb	Mar	Apr	May	Jun
Opening stock	200	250	400	300	150	100
Units produced	850	850	850	850	850	850
	1050	1100	1250	1150	1000	950
Units sold	800	700	950	1000	900	800
Closing stock	250	400	300	150	100	150

Any opening stock figure less than 200 would result in the stock at the end of May falling below 100 units, while any figure above 200 would mean that the firm was carrying unnecessarily high stocks.

Once the pattern of production has been laid down, it becomes possible to construct a **production cost budget**. This is a statement of the manufacturing costs month by month, rather like a series of summarized monthly Manufacturing Accounts. In the case we are considering, because an even flow of production is expected to be maintained, the cost figures for each month will be identical. Suppose that material costs are £12 per unit, direct labour £15 per unit and other directly variable expenses £8 per unit; the monthly budget would be shown as:

		£
Material		10200
Labour		12750
Variable expenses		6800
		29750

and each of these costs, multiplied by six, would appear in the firm's **master budget** drawn up for the period. The function of the master budget is, of course, to predict the firm's profit and to set out the firm's expected financial condition when the production process has been completed. It would therefore have to incorporate a number of other subsidiary budgets, among which would normally be budgets for cash, selling expenses, administration expenses, debtors and creditors. The most important of these is the **cash budget**.

The cash budget

In Chapter 8 we considered the firm's need to be able to account for the way it has used its funds over the past accounting year. It is even more important that it should be able to predict its flow of cash over the *coming* period. Planning a firm's trading activity involves decisions about the timing of cash expenditure, and these decisions must take account of expected changes in the firm's bank balance if liquidity problems are to be avoided. Cash budgeting makes it possible for the firm to know in good time if or when fresh funds will be needed, in the form of an authorized overdraft or a new share or debenture issue, and how much will be required.

Example 9.1. Let us suppose that, in addition to the information we already have on the firm we have been considering, we are told that:

(1) Half of the monthly sales are for cash. Debtors are allowed one month's credit and they owed £12000 at the end of December.

(2) The raw materials required for production are purchased at the beginning of the month in which they are used. Three-quarters are bought on credit terms for payment at the end of the following month. Creditors at the end of December are owed £6000.

(3) The firm intends purchasing a new machine for £40000 on 1 April. A cheque for £20000 interest on investments is expected to be received on 1 June.

(4) Direct wages and variable expenses are paid in the month in which they are incurred.

(5) Fixed costs of £2000 per month are expected and will be paid monthly. In addition, £1800 will be provided for depreciation over the six months.

(6) The firm has a credit balance at the bank of £7000 at the end of December.

(7) The manufactured articles are sold at £40 each.

Cash budget

	Jan	Feb	Mar	Apr	May	Jun
	£	£	£	£	£	£
Receipts						
Sales[1] Cash	16000	14000	19000	20000	18000	16000
Credit	12000	16000	14000	19000	20000	18000
Other income: Interest	–	–	–	–	–	20000
Total receipts	28000	30000	33000	39000	38000	54000
Payments						
Purchases[2] Cash	2550	2550	2550	2550	2550	2550
Credit	6000	7650	7650	7650	7650	7650
Wages	12750	12750	12750	12750	12750	12750
Variable expenses	6800	6800	6800	6800	6800	6800
Fixed expenses	2000	2000	2000	2000	2000	2000
Purchase of machine	–	–	–	40000	–	–
Total payments	30100	31750	31750	71750	31750	31750
Net receipts[3]	(2100)	(1750)	1250	(32750)	6250	22250
Bank balance b/forward[4]	7000	4900	3150	4400	(28350)	(22100)
Bank balance c/forward	4900	3150	4400	(28350)	(22100)	150

Notes
1. The total revenue from sales in January is £32000 (800 articles at £40). Half of this is from cash sales and therefore received in

January; the other is from credit sales payable in February. The credit sales income shown for January represents payments made by debtors for goods bought in December.

2. Purchases each month are £10 200 (850 units at £12). A quarter is paid in cash in the same month and the remainder is paid in the following month. The credit purchases shown for January are payments to creditors for materials bought in December.

3. The net receipts figure is arrived at by subtracting total payments from total receipts. In January and February, this is a negative figure.

4. The bank balance at the end of December is £7 000. When the negative net receipts figure for January is subtracted from this balance, the closing balance for the month is shown to be £4 900. This in turn becomes the opening balance for February.

Notice that no account has been taken of the depreciation of £1 800 provided for the period. This is because the provision does not involve a payment in cash and therefore does not affect the bank balance.

This cash budget, as it has been set out, reveals an expected overdraft of £28 350 in April, which would be cleared by the end of June. This would be a large overdraft to sustain considering the firm's scale of operations, and it is probable that management would prefer to raise the amount required from fresh share capital or from a loan issue, rather than seek an overdraft facility of this size from the bank. An inflow of funds received from either of these sources would be shown in the other income section of the cash budget and would automatically cancel the overdraft.

Break-even analysis

One of the most important preliminaries to the planning of production is the calculation of the point in the range of output at which the revenue from the sales of the firm's products will exactly equal the cost of making them. This is called the **break-even point**. Only by setting its target production above this point can the firm expect to make a profit.

We know from our analysis of the Manufacturing Account (see Chapter 4) that the cost structure of any product can be divided into two main sections: (a) *variable costs* – costs which represent direct inputs into each unit produced and which therefore will *vary directly* with the volume of production. Materials and labour are obvious examples of this type of cost; (b) *fixed costs or overheads* – costs which relate to the production, selling and administration process as a whole and which are not related directly to each unit produced. They will *vary with time* rather than with the volume of production. Examples of such costs are factory rent, wages of cleaners and depreciation of machinery.

The sales revenue which the company expects to receive from the production process as a whole must cover both these costs and still allow a reasonable margin of profit. Reduced to unit terms, however, this can be looked at a little differently. If the variable costs of a unit of a particular product which is sold for £50 are:

Materials	£18
Labour	£12

then, obviously, the difference between this variable cost of £30 and the selling price of the article represents a *contribution* towards the firm's fixed costs and profit. Now how much the sale of any particular article is contributing towards the recovery of fixed costs and how much towards profit will, in a sense, depend on where it occurs in the range of production. The entire proceeds from the first units produced will cover only the variable costs and a proportion of the fixed costs, and this will continue up to the break-even point; at this level of output, fixed costs will have been fully recovered. The determination of break-even point therefore becomes a matter of calculating how many contributions from individual units are required in order to recover the total amount of fixed costs. In the present case, articles which cost £30 in materials and labour and which are sold at £50 are making a contribution of £20 each towards fixed costs and profit. If the total fixed cost incurred in the production and sale of these articles is £7 500, then:

$$\text{Break-even point} = \frac{\text{Total fixed costs}}{\text{Contribution per unit}} = \frac{£7\,500}{£20} = 375 \text{ units}$$

The firm would have to produce and sell 375 units at a price of £50 each to avoid incurring a loss.

This can be demonstrated graphically by means of a **Break-even Chart**. The chart is constructed by:

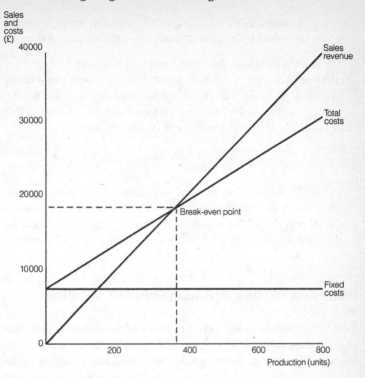

(i) Plotting sales revenue at the firm's full production (assumed to be 800 units here) and then connecting this point with the point of intersection of the two axes. This will show the firm's sales revenue at every level of production.

(ii) Plotting fixed costs at zero production and at full production and drawing a line to connect the two points. This line will be parallel to the volume of sales axis, indicating that fixed costs are constant at all levels of production.

(iii) Plotting the total cost (i.e. variable cost *plus* fixed cost) at full production and then connecting this point with the total cost point on the vertical axis (in this case £7 500, because fixed costs are incurred from the moment production begins). Break-even is the point of intersection between this total cost line and the sales revenue line. In this case it occurs at 375 units and £18750 revenue.

It will be seen from this chart that profit will be made at all levels of production between break-even point and maximum production. This section of the Sales Revenue line is called the *Margin of Safety*. It is sometimes expressed as a percentage of current revenue; in this case assuming the current revenue to be £40000, then:

$$\text{Margin of safety} = \frac{(£40000 - £18750)}{£40000} \times 100 = 53.125\%$$

The profit or loss at any level of production can be read from the chart by measuring the vertical distance between the total revenue and total cost lines. This is particularly useful when there is a need to discover the effect on profit of changes in costs or selling prices.

Marginal costing and management decisions

Break-even analysis is only one of the ways in which **marginal costing** methods assist management in its planning decisions. Marginal costing is distinguished from **absorption costing** by its treatment of fixed costs. Absorption costing proceeds by averaging the total costs of the firm, including fixed costs, over the number of units produced, thus *absorbing* the full cost of production into the cost of the individual units. This cost per unit is then deducted from the price to establish the profit per unit. This is a sound method of accounting when applied to historical information, but it is of limited usefulness in planning, because it does not take account of the effects of changes in volume of production on fixed costs per unit. Marginal costing, on the other hand, does not specifically attribute fixed costs to units of production; it regards the difference between the price of an article and its *marginal cost* (variable cost, seen as the cost of producing one extra unit at the margin of production) as a contribution towards both fixed cost and profit. The effect of this can be seen from the following example.

Example 9.2. A manufacturing concern has firm orders for the coming year for 10 000 items of a particular product at a selling price of £12 each. It estimates its variable cost at £5 per unit and total fixed expenses at £40 000. It is also considering an order from an overseas firm for a further 1 000 articles at a price of £8 each. Accepting this order would not depress the local selling price and it is within the firm's present capacity. Delivery expenses would be met by the customer. On an absorption basis, the total cost of each unit would be calculated as follows:

	Total £	Unit £
Variable cost	50 000	5.00
Fixed cost	40 000	4.00
	90 000	9.00

The selling price of the overseas order at £8 per unit would therefore be below the unit cost of £9. If the firm rejected the order on these grounds, however, it would be denying itself additional profit. As the order is within the firm's present capacity, no additional fixed costs would be involved. The difference between the marginal cost of the additional units (£5) and their selling price (£8) is therefore all profit and the firm would benefit to the extent of £3 000.

This, of course, is a simple example. In practice, the application of marginal costing techniques can be very difficult, especially where there is a widely variegated range of different lines being produced, or where there are changes of selling price or capacity at different levels of production.

Exercises

Exercise 9.1. The balance sheet of Great Expectations Ltd on 31 March 1986 is as follows:

	£	£	£
Assets			
Fixed assets at cost		20 000	
less: Depreciation		4 000	16 000
Current assets			
Stock		25 000	

Debtors		12000
Bank		5000
		42000

Current liabilities			
Creditors	20000		
Accrued rent	2000		
Proposed dividend	6000	28000	
Working capital			14000
			30000

Financed by:

30000 Ordinary shares of £1		30000

On the basis of this balance sheet and the following information, prepare a cash budget for the months of April, May and June.

(1)	Credit sales £	Cash sales £	Credit purchases £
March (actual)	12000	8000	20000
April (budgeted)	20000	10000	14000
May (budgeted)	24000	15000	15000
June (budgeted)	28000	18000	13000

(2) The proposed dividend will be paid in May.

(3) Trade creditors allow, and trade debtors are allowed, one month's credit.

(4) Wages £8000 and administration expenses £3000 will be paid in the month they are incurred. Rent of £2000 is paid one month in arrear.

(5) An asset costing £8000, and on which depreciation of £1000 has been allowed, is expected to be sold in April for £6000. A new asset costing £15000 will be purchased in June.

Exercise 9.2.   The Crystal Ball Co. Ltd is planning its operations for the coming year and expects the unit variable costs of its main product to be:

Materials	£8
Labour	£5

Each unit will be sold for £20 and total fixed costs will be £14 000. Full capacity is 5 000 units.

(a) Using a break-even chart, calculate: (i) the break-even point; and (ii) the number of units which will have to be sold to make a profit of £7 000.
(b) Check your answers, using the standard mathematical formulae.

10 Capital Investment Budgeting

The need for capital budgeting

One vital aspect of the prediction function has so far been touched upon only briefly. The resources which a firm commits to production in the way of direct materials, labour and indirect inputs represent only a part of the firm's investment. Trading generally, and manufacturing in particular, would not take place at all if firms did not also spend large sums of money on such fixed assets as premises, machinery and vehicles; and the extent to which these investment decisions are wisely made will have an important bearing on the firm's profitability. A single error in deciding upon a costly project, particularly if it involves specialized equipment, could have irreversible consequences which might seriously damage a company's prospects. This is why the responsibility for the purchase of fixed assets above a certain value is always reserved to senior management.

Methods of evaluation

The problem in capital investment decision-making is to select the most profitable project from among a number of competing alternatives. This involves comparing the amount of money which would be spent on each alternative asset with the income which would be expected to be derived from it; if project A which costs £300000 is expected to produce £400000, then the **net cash flow** would be calculated as £100000; if this exceeded the cash flow from

competing projects, A would be chosen. But, in practice, decisions
are nothing like as simple as this suggests. The typical pattern of
cash flows in capital budgeting is irregular, beginning with a large
single payment followed by a flow of income which is spread over
a number of years and may vary considerably from year to year.
The long-range planning of the purchase and use of fixed assets is
affected very much more by uncertainty and risk than is budgeting
for production and sales. A number of different techniques are
employed to minimize this risk, and these may be used either as
alternatives or in combination with one another.

The payback method

Because the cost of a fixed asset tends to be high in proportion to the total investment of the firm, the period of time which
will elapse before this cost can be recovered will always be an
important consideration in deciding between projects. The **payback
method** evaluates the available options on this basis.

Example 10.1.   Eldorado Ltd is considering two alternative investment projects, A and B. The initial outlays and expected cash flows
are as follows:

	A £	B £
Outlay:		
Year 1 – Cost	400 000	450 000
" 2 – Training	20 000	–
	420 000	450 000
Cash inflow:		
Year 1	100 000	90 000
" 2	150 000	130 000
" 3	170 000	180 000
" 4	80 000	200 000
	500 000	600 000

Calculate the payback period in each case.

Solution.   The whole cost of the investment in A is recovered by the
end of the third year (£100 000 + £150 0000 + £170 000 = £420 000).
The payback period is therefore three years. In the case of B, £400 000

has been paid back by the end of the third year and £50000 remains to be recovered from the cash flow during the fourth year. If this flow is even throughout the year, recovery will have taken place by the end of March, the first quarter (£200000 ÷ £50000 = 4). The payback period for B is therefore 3¼ years. If this is the sole test to be applied, project A will be chosen in preference to B.

Although this method does emphasize the need for early return of cash, which is particularly important for firms with liquidity problems, it does have the serious disadvantage of ignoring results after payback. It does not, therefore, really answer the question as to which is the more profitable investment. This becomes obvious when the total return to A is compared with the total return to B.

The average rate of return method

The average rate of return method attempts to take account of the *profit* accruing to the asset over its lifetime – which it assumes to be ascertainable by conventional accounting methods – and to express this profit as a percentage of the expenditure involved. Problems arise, however, as to how this expenditure is to be defined. Some firms choose to regard it as the original cost of the asset, while others prefer to look upon it as 'average capital employed', after taking account of the depreciation written off over the period. We shall be treating it in the latter sense.

Example 10.2.   Shangri La Ltd is attempting to choose between two assets, X and Y. The costs and profits associated with these assets are:

	X £	Y £
Original Cost: Year 1	40000	50000
Profits (after depreciation):		
Year 1	–	2000
" 2	3000	3000
" 3	6000	5000
" 4	6000	6000
" 5	3000	4000
	18000	20000

Calculate the average rate of return on each asset.

Solution.   Notice, first, that what we are dealing with here is *profit*, not cash flow.

Average capital employed is defined, for our purpose, as: the full original cost plus the depreciated value at the end of the period, divided by two, or:

$$\frac{\text{Asset value 1 Jan Year 1} + \text{Asset value 31 Dec Year 5}}{2}$$

Therefore:

	X £	Y £
Average capital employed	$\dfrac{40000+0}{2}$	$\dfrac{50000+0}{2}$
=	20 000	25 000
Average profit per year	$\dfrac{18000}{5}$	$\dfrac{20000}{5}$
=	3 600	4 000
Average rate of return	$\dfrac{3600 \times 100}{20000}$	$\dfrac{4000 \times 100}{25000}$
=	18%	16%

On this basis, asset X will be chosen as yielding the higher annual average rate of return, provided that a return of 18% is regarded as an acceptable rate, bearing in mind shareholders' expectations and the average return being earned by other comparable firms.

The discounted rate of return method

The difficulty about the average rate of return method is that it does not allow for the difference in value between profit earned in Year 1 and the same amount of profit earned in Year 5. Obviously £3 600 earned this year is of more value than the prospect of earning £3 600 in five years' time. This introduces the element of *interest*, which is the reward earned by an investor for deferring the satisfaction he could have gained from spending his money immediately. If the prevailing rate of interest is 10%, the investor knows that he could earn £3600 in five years' time by investing a considerably lower sum of money at compound interest; and this lower sum of money will represent the value of that profit to him now. The factor used in calculating the amount of investment required for this purpose is easily ascertainable from compound interest tables, but it might be as well, for a fuller understanding of the subject, to spend a little time considering the not too difficult arithmetic involved.

The standard formula for calculating the value of a sum of money invested at a particular rate of interest in a given number of years' time is:

$$A = P(1 + r)^n$$

where A is the value to be calculated, P is the sum invested, r the rate of interest and n the number of years. Thus the value of an investment of £100 at compound interest for three years at 5% will be:

$$£100(1 + 0.05)^3 = £115.7625$$

To calculate the *present value* of the investment which will produce £115.7625 in three years at 5%, the calculation is reversed and the formula becomes:

$$P = \frac{1}{(1 + r)^n} \times A$$

which is, of course, the reciprocal of our original formula. Thus:

$$\frac{1}{(1.05)^3} = 0.952^3 = 0.8638$$

and

$$£115.7625 \times 0.8638 = £100$$

The application of this formula to the determination of a rate of interest which will equate a cash flow over a number of years to the sum of money originally invested is a little more intricate.

Example 10.3.   Utopia Ltd is contemplating the purchase of an asset costing £380000 which is expected to generate the cash flow shown in the following schedule:

	Cash flow £
Year 1	90000
" 2	110000
" 3	120000
" 4	115000
" 5	170000
	605000

Calculate the discounted rate of return on the investment.

Solution. There is no simple and direct arithmetical method of establishing the rate of return. A process of trial and error will be involved, which will necessitate our experimenting with two or more discount rates. Let us select 15% for our first attempt.

Year	Cash flow £	Discounting factor at 15%	Present value £
1	90000	0.870	78300
2	110000	0.756	83160
3	120000	0.658	78960
4	115000	0.572	65780
5	170000	0.497	84490
	605000		390690

We have chosen too low a discount factor because if a cash flow of £605000 represents a return of 15% on an investment of £390690, it will represent a higher return on £380000. Let us now try 16%.

Year	Cash flow £	Discounting factor at 16%	Present value £
1	90000	0.862	77580
2	110000	0.743	81730
3	120000	0.641	76920
4	115000	0.552	63480
5	170000	0.476	80920
	605000		380630

From these calculations it can be seen that the discounted cash flow accruing to the firm from the purchase of the asset represents a return of 16% on its cost. Any competing option earning less than this would be rejected.

The net present value method

One of the considerations which firms have constantly to bear in mind when attempting to assess the profitability of investments is that the money which is expended on the purchase of assets has its own cost. This cost may be the interest payable on debentures, bank loans or other methods of raising funds; or it may be the 'opportunity cost' of the investment, that is, the return which it might have earned if it had been used in some other way. Because of this need to take account of the cost of finance, firms often lay down a required minimum rate of return on all investment projects and then rank projects according to the extent by which their total return, determined by this rate, exceeds their cost. This difference between return and cost is referred to as **net present value.**

Example 10.4. Rainbow Ltd wishes to replace a machine and is considering two models, one costing £50 000 and the other £60 000, each with a life-span of five years. From the following cash flow schedules, calculate the net present value at the required minimum rate of 14%.

	Cash Flow	
	Model A	*Model B*
	£	£
Year 1	9 000	15 000
" 2	17 000	18 000
" 3	23 000	20 000
" 4	20 000	28 000
" 5	15 000	22 000

Solution

Year		Model A		Model B	
	Discounting factor (14%)	Cash flow £	Present value £	Cash flow £	Present value £
1	0.877	9000	7893	15000	13155
2	0.770	17000	13090	18000	13860
3	0.675	23000	15525	20000	13500
4	0.592	20000	11840	28000	16576
5	0.519	15000	7785	22000	11418
			56133		68509
	Less cost of asset		50000		60000
	Net present values		6133		8509

Model B has the higher net present value and would therefore be chosen.

Exercise

Exercise 10.1.   Avalon Ltd is considering the relative merits of two projects costing £60000 and £80000 respectively. They are expected to generate the following cash flows:

		Project 1 £	Project 2 £
Year	1	19000	31000
"	2	21000	49000
"	3	30000	24000
"	4	18000	8000
"	5	9000	–

Calculate, for each project: (i) the payback period; (ii) the discounted rate of return; and (iii) the net present value, assuming a required minimum rate of return of 16%.

You will find the following present value table useful:

Year	15%	16%	18%	20%
1	0.870	0.862	0.847	0.833
2	0.756	0.743	0.718	0.694
3	0.658	0.641	0.609	0.579
4	0.572	0.552	0.516	0.482
5	0.497	0.476	0.437	0.402

5 The Control Function

11 Standard Costing and Budgetary Control

The need for controls

There is an element of control in almost everything an accountant does. We have seen in Chapter 3 how Control Accounts are used to check the postings to debtors' and creditors' personal accounts, and there are similar checks built in at every stage of the accounting process. It is in the context of planning, however, that the control function becomes most explicit. Control is a necessary complement to prediction because, unless there can be some certainty that production plans can be put into effect and that unforeseen developments in the production process can be detected and dealt with as they arise, budgeting becomes little more than an exercise in wishful thinking.

Standard costing

Budgetary control involves a continuing comparison of actual production with planned production. To make this comparison possible, it is necessary to develop a set of measurement standards for all the elements of cost. A **standard cost** is a predetermined cost calculated in relation to the working conditions which are expected to prevail during the budgeted period. Because standard costs are the basis on which production performance will be measured and adjustments will be made, their preparation requires great care and considerable technical expertise. They must also be set within a framework of what is realistically attainable so that, although a high level of competence is expected, allowance is also made for unavoidable waste and a reasonable margin of human imperfection. The standard cost of any product is made up of three elements: (i) the material cost, (ii) the labour cost, and (iii) the overhead cost apportioned to the product. Material cost itself is determined by two factors, both of which are variable: the (i) *price* of the input and (ii) its *usage*, that is the amount of material consumed in the production process. Thus, if the production of a single metal box is expected to require the input (or usage) of 2 lb. of metal at a price of £1.50 per lb., then obviously the material cost of each unit will be £3. Similarly, the labour cost is determined by both the *wage rate* and the *efficiency* of labour, that is the time taken to produce the unit. If the production of a metal box is expected to take 15 minutes of the time of a workman who is paid £5 an hour, then the labour element of the standard cost will be £1.25. Overhead costs cannot be attributed to individual units in the same way, precisely because they are *indirect* costs. A **standard rate** must first be calculated by dividing the total overhead cost by the number of labour hours, or machine hours, depending on which (labour or machine usage) is the predominating input into the production process. Thus, if the overhead cost for the production of all the metal boxes is £10 000 and the number of hours which will be worked is estimated at 5 000, then, if the manufacturing process is labour intensive, the standard rate will be set at: £10 000 ÷ 5 000 = £2 per hour. As the production of each box requires 15 minutes of labour time, the overhead cost absorbed into each unit will be £2 × 15/60, or £0.50. The composition of the standard cost for one metal box will therefore be:

Material cost = price × usage = 2 lb. × £1.50   = £3.00
Labour cost = rate × efficiency = £5.00 × 15/60   = £1.25
Overhead cost = time × standard rate = 15/60 × £2.00 = £0.50
Standard cost   £4.75

Variance analysis

The difference between a standard cost and the cost which is actually incurred is known ás a **variance**; this can be *adverse*, when it reflects an increase in cost, or *favourable*, when it reflects a decrease in cost. The process of production should be monitored constantly to detect significant adverse variances, so that the attention of management can be directed towards correcting them as quickly as possible. (This is an example of what is known as **management by exception**: the concentration of management attention on deviations from a standard, rather than on aggregates.)

Corrective action must, of course, be based on a close analysis of the variance. **Variance analysis**, although a simple enough technique in principle, can be extremely complicated in practice; in essence, it breaks down the variance into differences in the elements of standard cost and actual cost. This is best illustrated by means of a simple example:

Example 11.1. The following details have been extracted from the budget of a firm producing metal boxes.

Budgeted production:	20000 units
Standard quantity of materials:	40000 lb.
Standard price of materials:	£1.50 per lb.
Standard labour rate:	£5.00 per hour
Standard hours worked:	5000
Budgeted fixed overheads:	£10000

The following actual performance figures were recorded:

Production:	20000 units
Materials used:	44000 lb.
Price of materials:	£1.40 per lb.
Labour rate:	£5.50 per hour
Hours worked:	4500
Fixed overheads incurred:	£11000

Set out and explain the variances. (In the workings which follow, (*A*) denotes an adverse variance and (*F*) a favourable variance.)

Solution.   The first step is to calculate the total variance.

Total variance

	Budgeted cost £	Actual cost £	Variance £
Materials (price × quantity)	60 000	61 600	1 600 (A)
Labour (rate × hours)	25 000	24 750	250 (F)
Fixed overheads	10 000	11 000	1 000 (A)
	95 000	97 350	2 350 (A)

The total actual cost of production exceeds the total standard cost by £2 350 – an adverse variance. This total variance is made up of (i) an adverse material variance of £1 600; (ii) a favourable labour variance of £250, and (iii) an adverse fixed overhead variance of £1 000. These individual variances must now be examined.

Material variance

Material price variance = actual quantity × (standard price – actual price)
= 44 000 × (£1.50 − £1.40)   = £4 400 (F)

Usage variance = standard price × (standard quantity − actual quantity)
= £1.50 × (40 000 − 44 000)   = £6 000 (A)
£1 600 (A)

The actual price paid for the materials used in production was £1.40 per lb., 10 pence lower than the standard price. This resulted in a saving – or favourable variance – on the 44 000 lb. of materials actually used of £4 400. On the other hand, this actual quantity of materials used exceeded the standard set by 4 000 lb., which at the standard price of £1.50 resulted in an adverse variance of £6 000. The net effect of the favourable price variance of £4 400 and the adverse usage variance of £6 000 is an adverse total material variance of £1 600.

Labour variance

Labour rate variance = actual hours × (standard rate – actual rate)
= 4 500 × (£5.00 − £5.50)   = £2 250 (A)

Labour efficiency variance = standard rate × (standard hours − actual hours)
= £5.00 × (5 000 − 4 500)   = £2 500 (F)
£ 250 (F)

The actual time spent on the production of the budgeted number of boxes was 500 hours below the standard set. This increase in efficiency resulted in a favourable variance of £2500. However the wage rate was £0.50 higher than anticipated, resulting in a £2250 adverse variance. Together, these account for the net labour favourable variance of £250.

Overhead variance
From the information given, it is evident that the total overhead variance is £1000. The actual fixed costs incurred were £11000 as against the budgeted overhead of £10000, resulting in an *expenditure variance* of £1000 (A). In this question, since the budgeted production of 20000 units was actually attained, this is the only overhead variance that we need consider. However, if only 19000 units had actually been produced, we would also have had to take account of an adverse overhead *volume variance* of £500, because only £9500 (19000 × £0.50) of the standard overhead cost of £10000 would have been absorbed into the unit cost.

Other aspects of budgetary control

Budgetary control is a continuous activity, extending over all the operations of the business. It is therefore more than simply the detection, analysis and correction of variances. It is in many ways as much an attitude of mind as it is a set of technical procedures; and it will be successful only to the extent that it can draw upon the active participation of all the elements of the firm. Departmental and individual interests have to be aligned for the good of the organization as a whole. Accounting makes an important contribution to this *goal congruence* (as it is called technically) by providing a system of 'responsibility accounting' which allocates costs and revenues to the particular areas of responsibility of people to whom authority has been assigned, and thus enables their performance to be assessed.

Exercise

Exercise 11.1. A company planning the production of 1 000 units of a particular item calculated its unit standard costs as follows:

Materials: 10 lb. at £5.00 per lb.
Labour: 3 hours at £8.00 per hour

The target of 1 000 units was achieved, but the following units costs were recorded:

Materials: 11 lb. at £4.50 per lb.
Labour: 2.5 hours at £10.00 per hour

Calculate:

(a) the total variance
(b) (i) the material variance
    (ii) the material price variance
    (iii) the material usage variance
(c) (i) the labour variance
    (ii) the labour rate variance
    (iii) the labour efficiency variance.

Solutions to Exercises

Exercise 1.1.

Capital

		£			£
			Aug 1 Cash		5 000

Cash

		£			£
Aug 1	Capital	5 000	Aug 1	Purchases	1 500
" 2	Sales	50	" 3	Rent	400
" 3	Sales	150	" 5	Balance c/d	4 240
" 4	Sales	400			
" 5	J. D'Arcy	150			
	B. Cholmondeley	90			
	Sales	300			
		6 140			6 140
Aug 5	Balance b/d	4 240			

Purchases

		£			£
Aug 1	Cash	1 500	Aug 5	Balance c/d	2 000
" 4	Mayfair Wholesalers	500			
		2 000			2 000
Aug 5	Balance b/d	2 000			

Sales

		£			£
Aug 5 Balance c/d		1505	Aug 2 Cash		50
			J. D'Arcy		250
			" 3 Cash		150
			B. Cholmondeley		90
			" 4 S. Ponsonby		200
			R. Beauchamp		65
			" 5 Cash		400
			Cash		300
		1505			1505
			Aug 5 Balance b/d		1505

J. D'Arcy

		£			£
Aug 2 Sales		250	Aug 5 Cash		150
			Balance c/d		100
		250			250
Aug 5 Balance b/d		100			

Rent

		£		£
Aug 3 Cash		400		

B. Cholmondeley

		£			£
Aug 3 Sales		90	Aug 5 Cash		90

S. Ponsonby

		£		£
Aug 4 Sales		200		

R. Beauchamp

		£		£
Aug 5 Sales		65		

Mayfair Wholesalers

	£			£
		Aug 4 Purchases		500

Trial balance as at 5 August

	Dr	Cr
	£	£
Capital		5 000
Cash	4 240	
Purchases	2 000	
Sales		1 505
Rent	400	
J. D'Arcy	100	
S. Ponsonby	200	
R. Beauchamp	65	
Mayfair Wholesalers		500
	7 005	7 005

Exercise 1.2.

Capital

	£		£
		Sep 1 Cash	6 000

Cash

	£		£
Sep 1 Capital	6 000	Sep 3 Rent	400
" 2 Sales	550	Insurance	300
" 3 Sales	700	" 5 Wages	100
" 4 Sales	250	S. Uperman	1 000
S. Piderman	120	Balance c/d	6 120
" 5 Sales	300		
	7 920		7 920
Sep 5 Balance b/d	6 120		

Purchases

	£		£
Sep 1 S. Uperman	2 000		

Sales

	£		£
Sep 5 Balance c/d	2 120	Sep 2 Cash	550
		S. Piderman	120
		" 3 Cash	700
		" 4 Cash	250
		" 5 Cash	300
		C. Marvel	200
	2 120		2 120
		Sep 5 Balance b/d	2 120

S. Uperman

		£			£
Sep 5	Cash	1000	Sep 1	Purchases	2000
	Balance c/d	1000			
		2000			2000
			Sep 5	Balance b/d	1000

S. Piderman

		£			£
Sep 1	Sales	120	Sep 4	Cash	120

C. Marvel

		£		£
Sep 5	Sales	200		

Rent

		£		£
Sep 3	Cash	400		

Insurance

		£		£
Sep 3	Cash	300		

Wages

		£		£
Sep 5	Cash	100		

Trial balance as at 5 September

	Dr	Cr
	£	£
Capital		6000
Cash	6120	
Purchases	2000	
S. Uperman		1000
Sales		2120
Rent	400	
Wages	100	
C. Marvel	200	
Insurance	300	
	9120	9120

Exercise 2.1.

Cash Book

		Discount	Cash	Bank			Discount	Cash	Bank
		£	£	£			£	£	£
Sep	1 Balance b/d		900	8000	Sep	2 Rent		100	
	Sales		500			Bank		800	
"	2 L. John	44		836	"	3 F. Tuck	125		1125
	Sales		450		"	4 W. Scarlet			620
	Cash			800	"	5 Bank		500	
"	3 Sales		300			Wages		600	
"	4 R. Hood	27		513		Balance c/d		770	8904
	Sales		270						
"	5 Cash			500					
	Sales		350						
		71	2770	10649			125	2770	10649
Sep	5 Balance b/d		770	8904					

Sales Day Book

			Invoice No.	
				£
Sep	1	R. Hood	458	400
		A. Sheriff	459	650
"	3	M. Miller	460	300
				1350

Purchases Day Book

			Invoice No.	
				£
Sep	1	F. Tuck	928	500
		W. Scarlet	062	300
				800

Returns Inwards Book

			Note No.	
				£
Sep	3	R. Hood	57	80
		A. Sheriff	58	50
				130

Returns Outwards Book

		Note No.	£
Sep 4	F. Tuck	104	17
	A. Adale	105	23
			40

Journal

	Dr	Cr
	£	£
Office Equipment	400	
Nottingham Office Supplies		400
Purchase of typewriter – Suppliers' invoice 781/X		

General Ledger

Capital

	£			£
		Sep 1	Balance b/d	14000

Vehicles

		£		£
Sep 1	Balance b/d	5000		

Office Equipment

		£			£
Sep 1	Balance b/d	1000	Sep 5	Balance c/d	1400
" 5	Nottingham Office Supplies	400			
		1400			1400
Sep 5	Balance b/d	1400			

Sales

		£			£
Sep 5	Balance c/d	19220	Sep 1	Balance b/d	16000
			" 4	Cash	500
			" 2	Cash	450
			" 3	Cash	300
			" 4	Cash	270
			" 5	Cash	350
				Sundry Debtors	1350
		19220			19220
			Sep 5	Balance b/d	19220

Purchases

		£			£
Sep	1 Balance b/d	11 000	Sep	5 Balance c/d	11 800
"	3 Sundry Creditors	800			
		11 800			11 800
Sep	5 Balance b/d	11 800			

Returns Inwards

		£			£
Sep	1 Balance b/d	770	Sep	5 Balance c/d	900
"	3 Sundry Debtors	130			
		900			900
Sep	5 Balance b/d	900			

Returns Outwards

		£			£
Sep	5 Balance c/d	620	Sep	1 Balance b/d	580
			"	4 Sundry Creditors	40
		620			620
			Sep	5 Balance b/d	620

Discounts Allowed

		£			£
Sep	1 Balance b/d	1830	Sep	5 Balance c/d	1901
"	5 Sundry Debtors	71			
		1901			1901
Sep	5 Balance b/d	1901			

Discounts Received

		£			£
Sep	5 Balance c/d	1075	Sep	1 Balance b/d	950
			"	5 Sundry Creditors	125
		1075			1075
			Sep	5 Balance b/d	1075

Wages

		£			£
Sep	1 Balance b/d	1700	Sep	5 Balance c/d	2300
"	5 Cash	600			
		2300			2300
Sep	5 Balance b/d	2300			

Insurance

		£				£
Sep	1 Balance b/d	990				

Rent

		£				£
Sep	1 Balance b/d	600	Sep	5 Balance c/d		700
"	2 Cash	100				
		700				700
Sep	5 Balance b/d	700				

Nottingham Office Supplies

	£				£
		Sep	5 Office Equipment		400

Sales Ledger

R. Hood

		£				£
Sep	1 Balance b/d	540	Sep	3 Returns Inwards		80
	Sales	400	"	4 Bank		513
				Discount		27
				Balance c/d		320
		940				940
Sep	5 Balance b/d	320				

A. Sheriff

		£				£
Sep	1 Sales	650	Sep	3 Returns Inwards		50
			"	5 Balance c/d		600
		650				650
Sep	5 Balance b/d	600				

L. John

		£				£
Sep	1 Balance b/d	880	Sep	2 Bank		836
				Discount Allowed		44
		880				880

M. Miller

			£				£
Sep	1	Balance b/d	340	Sep	5	Balance c/d	640
"	3	Sales	300				
			640				640

| Sep | 5 | Balance b/d | 640 |

Purchases Ledger

F. Tuck

			£				£
Sep	3	Bank	1125	Sep	1	Balance b/d	1250
		Discount Received	125			Purchases	500
"	4	Returns Outwards	17				
"	5	Balance c/d	483				
			1750				1750

| Sep | 5 | Balance b/d | 483 |

W. Scarlet

			£				£
Sep	4	Bank	620	Sep	1	Balance b/d	620
"	5	Balance c/d	300	"	3	Purchases	300
			920				920

| Sep | 5 | Balance b/d | 300 |

A. Adale

			£				£
Sep	4	Returns Outwards	23	Sep	1	Balance b/d	150
"	5	Balance c/d	127				
			150				150

| Sep | 5 | Balance b/d | 127 |

Trial Balance as at 5 September

	Dr	Cr
	£	£
Cash	770	
Bank	8904	
Capital		14000
Vehicles	5000	
Office Equipment	1400	
Sales		19220
Purchases	11800	
Returns Inwards	900	
Returns Outwards		620
Discounts Allowed	1901	
Discounts Received		1075
Wages	2300	
Rent	700	
Insurance	990	
Nottingham Office Supplies		400
R. Hood	320	
A. Sheriff	600	
M. Miller	640	
F. Tuck		483
W. Scarlet		300
A. Adale		127
	36225	36225

Exercise 3.1.

Journal

	Dr	Cr
	£	£
(a) Discounts Allowed	13	
Suspense		13

Correction of omitted entry in the Discounts Allowed Account

(b) R. Stones	682	
D. Straits		682

Correction of entry of payment by D. Straits in R. Stones' Account

(c) Suspense	90	
Sales		90

Correction of error in the Sales total caused by incorrect carry forward

(d) Suspense	300	
Rent		300

Correction of overcast error

(e) Premises   3000
     Purchases   3000
Correction of error whereby the cost of materials used
in the extension of premises was debited to the
Purchases Account

(f) Suspense   108
     B. Rats   108
Correction of omission to record payment

Ledger

Suspense Account

	£		£
Sales	90		485
Rent	300		13
B. Rats	108		
	498		498

Exercise 3.2.

Sales Ledger Control Account

	£		£
Sales	75 300	Bank	69 520
		Discount Allowed	1 560
		Sales Returns	400
		Balance c/d	3 820
	75 300		75 300
Balance b/d	3 820		

Purchases Ledger Control Account

	£		£
Bank	47 100	Purchases	51 500
Discount Received	910		
Purchases Returns	250		
Balance c/d	3 240		
	51 500		51 500
		Balance b/d	3 240

The balance carried down on the Purchases Ledger Control Account differs
from the Purchases Ledger total balance. This points to an error, or errors,
in either the Control Account entries or the entries in creditors' personal
accounts.

Exercise 3.3.

Cash Book (Bank account)

	£		£
Balance b/d	561	Bank Charges	23
Credit transfer:		Standing Order –	
B. Little	200	Insurance	150
		Dishonoured	
		Cheque –	
		S. Ukridge	85
		Balance c/d	503
	761		761
Balance b/d	503		

Bank Reconciliation

		£	£
Amended Cash Book balance			503
add: Unpresented cheques – F. Widgeon		125	
O. Prosser		270	395
			898
less: Unrecorded deposit			109
Balance as per bank statement			789

Exercise 4.1.

First In, First Out

	Purchases		Issues		Balance		
	Quantity	Price £	Quantity	Price £	Quantity	Price £	Value £
March	500	8	–	–	500	8	4 000
April	–	–	300	8	200	8	1 600
June	400	10	–	–	{ 200	8	5 600
					{ 400	10	
July	–	–	{ 200	8	200	10	2 000
			{ 200	10			
August	300	12	–	–	{ 200	10	5 600
					{ 300	12	
September	–	–	{ 200	10	200	12	2 400
			{ 100	12			

Last In, First Out

	Purchases		Issues		Balance		
	Quantity	Price £	Quantity	Price £	Quantity	Price £	Value £
March	500	8	–	–	500	8	4000
April	–	–	300	80	200	8	1600
June	400	10	–	–	{ 200	8	5600
					{ 400	10	
July	–	–	400	10	200	8	1600
August	300	12	–	–	{ 200	8	5200
					{ 300	12	
September	–	–	300	12	200	8	1600

Average Cost

	Purchases		Issues		Balance		
	Quantity	Price £	Quantity	Price £	Quantity	Price £	Value £
March	500	8	–	–	500	8	4000
April	–	–	300	8	200	8	1600
June	400	10	–	–	600	9.33	5600
July	–	–	400	9.33	200	9.33	1867
August	300	12	–	–	500	10.93	5467
September	–	–	300	10.93	200	10.93	2188

Total purchases are:
```
500 × £8  = £4000
400 × £10 =  4000
300 × £12 =  3600
             11600
```

	FIFO £	LIFO £	AVCO £
Purchases	11600	11600	11600
less: Closing stock	2400	1600	2188
Cost of goods sold	9200	10000	9412

Total sales are 1000 × £15 = £15000
Therefore:

	FIFO £	LIFO £	AVCO £
Sales	15000	15000	15000
less: Cost of goods sold	9200	10000	9412
Gross profit	5800	5000	5588

Exercise 4.2.

Manufacturing Account of Artoo Ltd
for year ended 30 June 1985

	£	£
Raw materials		
Stock at 1 July 1984	28450	
Purchases	78600	
	107050	
less: Stock at 30 June 1985	23210	
Cost of materials consumed		83840
Direct wages		61200
Prime cost		145040
Factory fuel and power		8300
Rent		2400
		155740
add: Work-in-progress 1 July 1984		3360
		159100
less: Work-in-progress 3 June 1985		1840
Cost of goods produced		157260

Trading Account of Artoo Ltd
for year ended 30 June 1985

	£	£
Sales		250100
Opening stock of finished goods	20500	
Cost of goods produced	157260	
	177760	
less: Closing stock of finished goods	17800	
Cost of goods sold		159960
		90140

Notice that the part of the Rent expense, £1200, which is not charged to the Manufacturing Account is also not included in the Trading Account. As we shall see in the next chapter, this is an item which will appear in the Profit and Loss Account.

Exercise 5.1.

**Profit and Loss Account
for year ended 31 December 1985**

	£	£	£
Gross profit			45 000
Discounts received			800
			45 800
Office salaries		12 000	
General expenses	9 000		
add: Accrued	300	9 300	
Discounts Allowed		650	
Provision for Doubtful Debts[1]		150	
Insurance[2]	600		
less: Prepaid	150	450	
Provision for Depreciation		800	23 350
Net profit			22 450

Workings:

(1) The Provision for Doubtful Debts shows a balance brought forward of £300. 5% of the debtors' figure is £450, so a further £150 must be provided.

(2) The annual insurance payment extends over a period which includes three months of the following year. Only three-quarters of the expense must therefore be charged against the current year's profit.

Exercise 5.2.

This solution has been prepared on the basis of the straight-line method of depreciation. It should be noticed, however, that the wording of the question does not exclude an answer presented on a reducing balance basis. The advantage of the straight line method in this case is that it makes it possible to confine the ledger account entries to the single year ending 31 March 1986.

Machinery

		£			£
1985			1985		
Apr 1 Balance b/d		20 000	Jul 1 Disposals		8 000
			1986		
			Mar 31 Balance c/d		12 000
		20 000			20 000
1986					
Mar 31 Balance b/d		12 000			

Provision for Depreciation

	£			£
1985		1985		
Jul 1 Disposals	5 200[2]	Apr 1 Balance b/d		15 000[1]
1986		1986		
Mar 31 Balance c/d	12 600	Mar 31 Profit and Loss		2 800[3]
	17 800			17 800
		1986		
		Mar 31 Balance b/d		12 600

Disposals

	£			£
1985		1985		
Jul 1 Machinery	8 000	Jul 1 Bank		1 500
		Provision for		
		Depreciation		5 200
		Profit and Loss		1 300
	8 000			8 000

The loss incurred in disposal of the asset is £1 300.

Workings:

(1) The credit balance brought forward on 1 April 1985 represents three years' depreciation at 20%.

(2) The amount transferred from the Provision for Depreciation to the Disposals Account is made up as follows:

20% of £8 000 for 3 years	4 800
$\frac{1}{4} \times$ 20% of £8 000 for 1 April to 30 June 1985	400
	5 200

(3) The current year's depreciation charge to Profit and Loss is calculated as follow:

3 months $\times$ 20% $\times$ £20 000 = £1 000	
9 months $\times$ 20% $\times$ £12 000 = 1 800	
	2 800

Exercise 6.1.

Appropriation Account

		£	£
Net profit			10000
add: Interest on drawings: Jerome		100	
George		50	
Harris		45	195
			10195
less: Interest on capital: Jerome		1500	
George		750	
Harris		500	2750
			7445
less: Salary: Harris			2000
			5445
less: Share of profit: Jerome		3267	
George		1089	
Harris		1089	5445

Capital: Jerome

		£			£
1984			1984		
Dec 31	Drawings	4000	Jan 1	Balance b/d	30000
	Interest on		Dec 31	Appropriation:	
	drawings	100		Interest on capital	1500
	Balance c/d	30667		Profit	3267
		34767			34767
				Balance b/d	30667

Capital: George

		£			£
1984			1984		
Dec 31	Drawings	2000	Jan 1	Balance b/d	15000
	Interest on		Dec 31	Appropriation:	
	drawings	50		Interest on capital	750
	Balance c/d	14789		Profit	1089
		16839			16839
				Balance b/d	14789

Capital: Harris

		£			£
1984			1984		
Dec 31	Drawings	1800	Jan 1	Balance b/d	10000
	Interest on			Appropriation:	
	drawings	45		Interest on capital	500
	Balance c/d	11744		Salary	2000
				Profit	1089
		13589			13589
				Balance b/d	11744

Balance sheet of Jerome, George and Harris as at 31 December 1984

	£	£	£
Capital: Jerome		30667	
George		14789	
Harris		11744	57200
Loan: Montmorency			5000
Current Liabilities: Creditors			2000
			64200

Assets	Cost	Depreciation	Net value
Fixed Assets: Equipment	29000	6000	23000
Vehicles	15000	4000	11000
	44000	10000	34000
Current Assets: Stock		19000	
Debtors	8000		
less: Provision for doubtful debts	150	7850	
Prepaid insurance		350	
Bank		3000	30200
			64200

Exercise 6.2.

Appropriation Account

	£	£
Net profit		80000
less: Transfer to General Reserve	10000	
Proposed preference dividend	2000	
Proposed ordinary dividend	15000	27000
Unappropriated profit (retained earnings)		53000

Dombey and Son Ltd
Balance Sheet as at 30 June 1985

	£	£	£
Capital and liabilities			
Authorized share capital			
40000 10% preference shares of £1 each			40000
100000 ordinary shares of £1 each			100000
			140000
Issued Share Capital			
20000 10% preference shares of £1 each			20000
100000 ordinary shares of £1 each			100000
			120000

Reserves		
Share premium	30000	
General Reserve	33000	
Retained earnings	53000	116000
		236000
12% Debentures		75000
		311000
Current Liabilities		
Creditors	22000	
Proposed dividends	17000	39000
		350000

Assets

Fixed Assets	Cost	Depreciation	Net Value
Premises	230000	–	230000
Vehicles	70000	3500	66500
	300000	3500	296500

Current assets			
Stock		15000	
Debtors	36200		
less: Provision for doubtful debts	1500		
	34700		
less: Provision for discounts	1200	33500	
Bank		5000	53500
			350000

Exercise 7.1.
Workings

	ABC Ltd	XYZ Ltd
	£	£
Sales	1300000	1600000
Cost of goods sold	900000	1000000
Gross profit	400000	600000
Expenses	290000	420000
Net profit	110000	180000

Return on capital employed $\frac{110000}{500000} \times 100 = 22.0\%$ $\frac{180000}{650000} \times 100 = 27.7\%$

Net profit percentage $\frac{110000}{1300000} \times 100 = 8.5\%$ $\frac{180000}{1600000} \times 100 = 11.3\%$

Gross profit percentage $\frac{400000}{1300000} \times 100 = 30.8\%$ $\frac{600000}{1600000} \times 100 = 37.5\%$

Selling expenses percentage $\frac{180000}{1300000} \times 100 = 13.9\%$ $\frac{240000}{1600000} \times 100 = 15.0\%$

Administration expenses percentage $\dfrac{110\,000}{1\,300\,000} \times 100 = 8.4\%$ $\dfrac{180\,000}{1\,600\,000} \times 100 = 11.25\%$

Asset turnover $\dfrac{1\,300\,000}{500\,000} = 2.60$ $\dfrac{1\,600\,000}{650\,000} = 2.46$

Fixed asset turnover $\dfrac{1\,300\,000}{370\,000} = 3.51$ $\dfrac{1\,600\,000}{480\,000} = 3.33$

Stock turnover rate $\dfrac{900\,000}{(100\,000 + 80\,000) \div 2} = 10$ $\dfrac{1\,000\,000}{(220\,000 + 280\,000) \div 2} = 4$

Debtor turnover $\dfrac{1\,000\,000}{(120\,000 + 130\,000) \div 2} = 8$ $\dfrac{1\,500\,000}{(140\,000 + 160\,000) \div 2} = 10$

Liquidity ratios

Working capital ratio $\dfrac{250\,000}{120\,000} = 2.08$ $\dfrac{440\,000}{270\,000} = 1.63$

Liquid ratio $\dfrac{250\,000 - 80\,000}{120\,000} = 1.42$ $\dfrac{440\,000 - 280\,000}{270\,000} = 0.59$

Investment ratios

Earnings per ordinary share $\dfrac{110\,000 - 10\,000}{300\,000} = 33.3$ pence $\dfrac{180\,000}{500\,000} = 36$ pence

(Note: in the case of ABC Ltd, the return due to the preference shareholders must be taken into account when calculating the return accruing to ordinary shareholders)

Dividend for ordinary shares $\dfrac{60\,000}{300\,000} = 20$ pence $\dfrac{150\,000}{500\,000} = 30$ pence

These calculations show XYZ to have a higher return on capital and net profit percentage, and a higher earnings per share and dividend rate. Before making his final decision, however, Mr Jones should consider the following points:

(1) XYZ's higher net profit is entirely a result of its lower cost of goods sold, as can be seen by comparing the two gross profit percentages. If there should be an increase in the cost of the firm's purchases relative to its sales for some reason outside the firm's control, its profit advantage over ABC would be significantly altered.

(2) XYZ Ltd's high selling expense percentage is probably connected with its very high level of stocks. Warehousing costs must be considerably greater than those for ABC Ltd. ABC's lower administration expenses can probably be accounted for, to some extent, by the fact that it owns its own premises and would therefore not, unlike XYZ, have to pay out large amounts in rent.

(3) XYZ's liquidity position is considerably worse than ABC's. Although its working capital ratio seems satisfactory at 1.63, the company appears very vulnerable when account is taken of its slow-moving stocks, its high creditors and its bank overdraft. This is reflected in an alarmingly low liquid ratio of 0.59.

(4) Out of its net profit of £110000, ABC has paid out £70000 in dividends and retained £40000 in its reserves. XYZ has paid out most of its net profit for the past year and added little to its reserves, which seems an unwise course of action in view of its liquidity position.

Overall, Mr Jones would probably be better advised to resist the specious attractiveness of XYZ's profit record. ABC, apart from being more stable, also seems in a better position for future expansion.

Exercise 8.1.

Statement of Sources and Applications of Funds

	£	£	£
Sources			
Profit from trading	10000		
add: Depreciation[1]	7000		
less: Profit on disposal[2]	(2000)		15000
Proceeds of sale of asset			12000
			27000
Applications			
Drawings	12000		
Purchase of asset[3]	29000		
Repayment of loan	5000		46000
Excess of applications over sources			19000
Increases/Decreases in working capital			
Increase in stock		5000	
Decrease in debtors		(3000)	
Increase in creditors[4]		(4000)	
Decrease in bank		(17000)	19000
Net decrease in working capital			

Notes

1. The annual charge to Profit and Loss for depreciation cannot be calculated simply by deducting the figure for 1985 from that for 1986, because the amount provided for the asset which has been sold has been transferred to the Disposals Account. It will be necessary to draw up a Provision for Depreciation Account.

Provision for Depreciation

	£		£
Disposals	5 000	Balance b/d	16 000
Balance	18 000	Profit and Loss	7 000
	23 000		23 000

After taking account of an opening balance of £16 000, a transfer to the Disposals Account of £5 000 and a closing balance of £18 000, it becomes apparent that £7 000 must have been transferred from the Profit and Loss Account.

2. The profit on disposal which has been credited to the Profit and Loss Account can be ascertained by writing up the Disposals Account.

Disposals

	£		£
Fixed assets	15 000	Bank	12 000
Profit and loss	2 000	Depreciation	5 000
	17 000		17 000

The profit of £2 000 must now be deducted from the Profit from Trading in order to avoid counting it in twice as a source of funds. The proceeds from the sale of the asset (£12 000) already include it.

3. The Fixed Assets Account must be written up to determine the amount of money expended on new assets during the year.

Fixed Assets

	£		£
Balance b/d	92 000	Disposals	15 000
Bank	29 000	Balance c/d	106 000
	121 000		121 000

If the closing balance is £106 000 after deduction of the disposal of £15 000, then the difference between this amount and the opening balance of £92 000 must represent the value of assets purchased during the year: £29 000.

4. The increase in creditors of £4 000 is a *decrease* in working capital.

Mr Micawber is in difficulties because: (i) his drawings have exceeded his net profit for the year; (ii) he has purchased assets which cost him £17 000 more than the proceeds from the sale of his old assets; and (iii) he has repaid £5 000 of the loan without making provision for fresh funds from other sources.

Exercise 9.1.

Cash Budget

	April £	May £	June £
Receipts			
Sales: Cash	10000	15000	18000
Credit[1]	12000	20000	24000
Sale of asset	6000	–	–
	28000	35000	42000
Payments			
Purchases[2]	20000	14000	15000
Wages	8000	8000	8000
Administration	3000	3000	3000
Rent[3]	2000	2000	2000
Purchase of asset	–	–	15000
Payment of dividend	–	6000	–
	33000	33000	43000
Net receipts	(5000)	2000	1000
Balance brought forward	5000	–	2000
Balance carried forward	–	2000	3000

Notes

1. Debtors are allowed one month's credit. The receipts for credit sales in April will, therefore, be (if debtors pay up promptly) the £12000 appearing against the debtors item in the balance sheet.
2. Creditors allow one month's credit. The £20000 shown as due to creditors in the balance sheet will therefore have to be paid in April.
3. Rent is payable in arrear. The £2000 shown as rent accrued in the balance sheet will therefore be paid in April.

Exercise 9.2.

(a) To construct the break-even chart: (i) Draw the fixed cost line parallel to the horizontal axis at £14000. (ii) Plot the sales revenue for 5000 units (£100000) and connect this point with the zero production point at the intersection of the two axes. (iii) Plot the total cost for 5000 units (fixed costs £14000 + variable costs £65000 = £79000) and connect this with the fixed cost point in the vertical axis. The point of intersection of the total cost line with the sales revenue line will be found to occur at 2000 units and £40000 revenue.

To find the level of production at which £7000 profit will be made, establish the point on the horizontal axis at which the vertical distance between the total cost line and the sales revenue line is exactly £7000. This will be found to be 3000 units.

(b) The formula for the calculation of break-even point is:

$$\frac{\text{Total fixed costs}}{\text{Contribution per unit}}$$

Contribution per unit is selling price − variable cost per unit. Therefore

$$\text{break-even point} = \frac{£14\,000}{£20 - £13} = 2\,000 \text{ units}$$

To establish the production necessary to ensure a profit of £7 000, calculate how many more contributions per unit will be required to make up £7 000.

$$\frac{\text{Total fixed cost + Profit required}}{\text{Contribution per unit}}$$

$$= \frac{£14\,000 + £7\,000}{£20 - £13} = 3\,000 \text{ units}$$

The required production level is therefore 3 000 units, 1 000 units above break-even point.

Exercise 10.1.

(i) *Payback period*

	Project 1 £	Project 2 £
Initial cost	60 000	80 000
Cost recovered:		
Year 1	19 000	31 000
2	21 000	49 000
3	20 000	−
	60 000	80 000

The payback period for Project 1 is 2 years + 20 000/30 000 of Year 3, that is, two years and eight months. For Project 2 it is exactly two years. On this basis, Project 2 would be preferred.

(ii) *Discounted rate of return*
We shall begin by testing both projects for a return of 20%.

		Project 1		Project 2	
Year	Discount factor at 20%	Cash flow £	Present value £	Cash flow £	Present value £
1	0.833	19 000	15 827	31 000	25 823
2	0.694	21 000	14 574	49 000	34 006
3	0.579	30 000	17 370	24 000	13 896
4	0.482	18 000	8 676	8 000	3 856
5	0.402	9 000	3 618	−	−
		97 000	60 065	112 000	77 581

For Project 1, 20% discounts a cash flow of £97 000 back to £60 065, which is as close to £60 000 as need concern us. However, a rate of 20% obviously does not fit Project 2. Let us now try 18% for Project 2.

Year	Discount factor at 18%	Cash flow £	Present value £
1	0.847	31 000	26 257
2	0.718	49 000	35 182
3	0.609	24 000	14 616
4	0.516	8 000	4 128
		112 000	80 183

This is as close as we shall get to £80 000 with a whole-number percentage rate. On this basis, Project 1 with a rate of return of 20% would be preferred to Project 2.

(iii) *Net present value*
The required minimum rate of return is 16%.

		Project A		Project B	
Year	Discount factor at 16%	Cash flow £	Present value £	Cash flow £	Present value £
1	0.862	19 000	16 378	31 000	26 722
2	0.743	21 000	15 603	49 000	36 407
3	0.641	30 000	19 230	24 000	15 384
4	0.552	18 000	9 936	8 000	4 416
5	0.476	9 000	4 284	–	–
			65 431		82 929
	Less cost of asset		60 000		80 000
	Net present value		5 431		2 929

Project 1 would be preferred as having the higher net present value.

Exercise 11.1.

(a) Total variance:

	£	£
Budgeted cost:		
Materials: 10 lb. at £5 × 1000	50 000	
Labour: 3 hours at £8 × 1000	24 000	74 000
Actual cost:		
Materials: 11 lb. at £4.50 × 1000	49 500	
Labour: 2.5 hours at £10 × 1000	25 000	74 500
		500 (A)

(b) (i) Material variance = standard material cost − actual material cost. These figures have already been calculated in (a) above, so:

$$£50 000 − £49 500 = £500(F)$$

(ii) Material price variance = actual quantity × (standard price − actual price)

$$= 11 000 \text{ lb.} × (£5.00 − £4.50)$$
$$= £5 500 \ (F)$$

(iii) Material usage variance = standard price × (standard quantity − actual quantity)

$$= £5 × (10 000 \text{ lb.} − 11 000 \text{ lb.})$$
$$= £5 000 \ (A)$$

Test: Material variance = Material price variance + Material usage variance

$$£500(F) = £5 500(F) + £5 000 \ (A)$$

(c) (i) Labour variance = standard labour cost − actual labour cost
Therefore, as in (a) above:

$$£24 000 − £25 000 = £1 000 \ (A)$$

(ii) Labour rate variance = actual hours × (standard rate − actual rate)
$$= 2 500 \text{ hours} × (£8.00 − £10.00)$$
$$= £5 000 \ (A)$$

(iii) Labour efficiency variance = standard rate × (standard hours − actual hours)

$$= £8 × (3 000 \text{ hours} − 2 500 \text{ hours})$$
$$= £4 000 \ (F)$$

Test: Labour variance = Labour rate variance + Labour efficiency variance
$$£1 000 \ (A) = £5 000 \ (A) + £4 000 \ (F)$$

Index